DEFEATING NARCISSISM

Looking Inside Dark Psychology and Manipulation to Learn About Narcissistic Personality Disorder and Breaking Free of Its Codependency

Broken Pen Publishing

Table of Contents

Introduction

Living with a narcissist can be a nightmare! Yes, it may sound a bit harsh, but it's true, and it's always better to face the truth head-on rather than keep denying it. If you've to deal with narcissism in your life to an extent that it ruins your mental wellbeing on a daily basis and keeps you from growing as an individual, it's time to take some serious action. You can't be passive about it. Although many of us have some narcissistic traits or the other, they are tolerable. It's always easier to tackle something while we have it faintly within us. But if something dominates your life completely, you need to get out of it before it overpowers you! Everybody deserves to be happy and so do you.

You may ignore a narcissistic person if they aren't related to you or somebody you're briefly associated with (bosses or colleagues). But if you constantly feel harassed, manipulated, and belittled by your parents, spouse, siblings, or friends, you need to approach the problem face to face. It may be hard, but not as hard as undergoing it relentlessly without a cure. You need to come to terms with the fact that it's unfair to allow other people to mistreat you in any manner, no matter how much they claim to love you. If you ought to be kind to others, you need to reserve that kindness for yourself, too. Narcissism can be tricky, as most of the time people who suffer from the narcissistic behaviors of others aren't even aware of it until they reach a point when they realize that their world is falling apart. Most of the time, the person with narcissism syndrome does not know that they're being hurtful to other people. They believe they're always right and nobody should disagree with them. Thus, when you spend too much time with such a personality, you feel humiliated, confused, and apologetic for no reason. It's as if you face punishment at no fault of your own. Neither you nor your relationship with that person gets any space to blossom. The more intimate your relationship is with that person, the more complicated the whole situation gets, and it's always extremely hard to part ways with someone you love. The worst part is that you feel more helpless because you don't want to confront that person, fearing they may hurt you, even more, when you tell them the truth.

When you allow narcissism to prevail over your life, it leads to depression, anxiety, hatred, and a myriad of bodily ailments. Don't let it become a lifelong battle, but choose to face it early on. If you delay dealing with narcissism, it's going to become more intense. It's never easy to deal with someone who has mental issues, but it's definitely harder to live with them. You need to be confident, positive, and self-reliant to overcome narcissism and end its codependency.

If you're stuck with a narcissistic person, you're not alone. To begin with, you need to believe that you are who you are, no matter what they say about you or how they make you feel. Your self-worth is independent of their opinions and behaviors. So, you need to love yourself and value your personal well-being and growth. Remember, loving somebody doesn't mean you need to lose your own identity. You're not meant to live in constant fear of saying or doing something to upset your narcissistic partner. You're free to express your own ideas and practice what you believe in rather than follow somebody else's advice and instructions all the time. You need to break the chain of "narcissistic" slavery that you feel trapped in. While you can't really change somebody else, you can definitely learn to deal with them and protect your sanity. Also, cutting ties with a narcissistic person isn't a rule. If you choose to keep the relationship (which is not always possible), it is possible to coexist with them and grow together. But you have to decide to use certain tactics to defend yourself and not let the other person's narcissistic ways harm you.

This book is going to help you identify the real-life tactics that narcissistic individuals use to manipulate people around them and also why they use them. To deal with narcissism, you must also understand the causes of its origin. You need to know what creates a narcissist. You need to comprehend the psychology behind narcissistic behavior to tackle it in a manner that you're able to retain your joy and peace.

The deeper you get into narcissism and uncover its many facets, the sooner you'll be able to escape its negative effects on your life. Awareness is the stepping stone toward any healing or recovery. If you've been through covert emotional and mental abuse, you'll know how to rise above it. You will also learn if manipulation can be positive sometimes and if it can possibly help you live with and change a narcissist if they are willing. However, you don't have to take responsibility for someone else's behavior or choices. You need to safeguard your life and individuality.

At the end of it, you will be able to fight the psychologically damaging situations caused by narcissism and achieve mental freedom. You don't have to doubt yourself or feel guilty about anything. Remember, the onus of maintaining harmony in a relationship is not solely on you. It needs to be shared by your other half, too. So, if you're doing your best and the other person isn't accommodating, you don't have to stretch yourself beyond a point.

Be aware, this book isn't written to tell you how to change a narcissist and their attitude. You can't really change another person, no matter how hard you try. You can help a person, guide them, and offer them emotional support, but you can't rewire their brain. So, don't even get there. The purpose of this book is to help you understand that *you* are important and that narcissism shouldn't defeat you. The journey of battling narcissism can be exhaustive and painful, but as long as you stand up for yourself, it can prove to be worthwhile, eventually.

Chapter 1:
What Creates the Shroud

Narcissists live in their own world. It's hard for them to glance beyond their pretentious self-image. The core quality of a narcissist is conceitedness. All they care for is themselves and their needs. They constantly want to boast about their abilities, talents, and achievements, which may or may not exist. They don't care about what other people think, feel, or want. In any given scenario, a narcissist wants to be celebrated blatantly. They feel entitled to criticize, mock, and degrade anyone. However, they aren't able to take even healthy criticism in stride. They also lack empathy because they have no intent to understand other people's feelings, thoughts, and emotions. To a narcissist, their opinion or analysis on a matter is the final word. If you get into a debate with them, you're inviting a lot of distress for yourself.

Before we learn about what creates a narcissist and everything else about it, let's understand that narcissism is quite a misunderstood term. It's not really about self-love. A narcissistic person doesn't really love themselves. They have no self-confidence. In fact, they loathe themselves, which is why they try to project themselves as brash, outgoing, intelligent, witty, and good-looking. They want to hide their "real" self from the world because they have the fear of being attacked on an emotional and mental level.

Narcissists falsely assume that there's nobody better than them and that they deserve relentless praise and acknowledgment from everyone. The reason behind their unending urge for admiration is their fragile ego, which can be shattered at any moment. They appear to be haughty and confident from the outside, but they have no real self-belief from the inside.

Self-love, in the right measure, is actually good for a person. It can become problematic if it enslaves an individual's personality. If you love yourself and have a high self-esteem, it can take you places. You can turn out to be a confident individual and can achieve whatever you seek in life. On the other hand, if you try to be too selfless and self-deprecating, it's not good for you, either. There has to be a good balance between knowing your worth and valuing others for who they are. When a person tilts toward being too prideful or too self-critical, it can indicate a personality disorder.

If a person thinks too highly of themselves, they are likely to fail in their relationships, career, finances, and every other aspect of their lives because they aren't able to consider the interests of others. Extremity of any kind is always unhealthy. Being a narcissist means to love thyself over everything else. When you do that, it stops your own growth as an individual and it keeps you from enjoying fulfilling relationships.

Narcissism is viewed on a spectrum, meaning it's not necessary for a narcissist to have all the symptoms. Some people may have mild narcissism and they may not even require any treatment or therapy. However, there's something called narcissistic personality disorder (NPD), which can create havoc in a person's life if it's not tackled properly and in a timely manner. It's a kind of mental condition that makes a person incapable of doing well in their career, social, and personal life. It's an occupational and social impairment, which needs immediate attention.

It's quite possible to have at least one narcissist in your family, social circle, or workplace. However, you may or may not get to know it. There are people who have narcissistic traits, but they manage to lead a normal life requiring no treatment. They can possibly have happy relationships, too. However, there are people who are on the higher side of the spectrum and they have quite a lot of evident narcissistic characteristics in them, which impact their life and the lives of others around them.

Are You Dealing With a Narcissist?

To know if you're living with a narcissist or have to deal with narcissism predominantly, you need to identify the following signs and symptoms in a person:

- A sense of superiority and pride. It's impossible for a narcissist to accept that somebody else can surpass them in intellect, knowledge, appearance, skills, and smartness. In their heads, narcissists are always on top and they're the most competent ones.
- They want to control everything and everyone. If things don't go according to their wishes, they get agitated fast because they believe they are always right. If you disagree with them about anything, they take it as a personal offense.
- They like to be associated with only high-profile people and tend to look down upon those of low status.
- They don't shy away from manipulating others for their own vested interests.
- They always look for attention, approval, and validation from others to keep their self-esteem thumping. If they feel you're not paying them enough attention and not making them feel loved, they make sure to pester you to shower more praise over them.
- They always seek perfection in situations and people, which is an unrealistic expectation. Thus, it gives them a chance to feel even more dissatisfied and angry.
- They also think that they have the right to judge how other people behave or what they choose to do. Therefore, they try to be moral teachers to whoever they find isn't acting according to their standards.
- They often envy others but have this impression that others are envious of them.

- They fail to take responsibility for their actions. If something goes wrong or if you try to confront them about a matter, they like to shift the blame onto you or somebody else.

Now that you know how to recognize narcissistic behavior in a person, you should also dig into its roots. Although the causes of narcissistic behavior are quite unfathomable, factors like imbalanced parenting, genetics, or neurobiology are likely to be responsible for the same.

You should also know that some people are born narcissists. Even if someone is a narcissist because they were raised in a particular environment and had a certain upbringing, there's still a bit of it which is inherent in them. While we're going to look at the possible causes of narcissism, they aren't an excuse to let go of any narcissistic abuse by anybody. The purpose of knowing how narcissism can emerge in a person is to be able to find a solution and an escape door.

Parenting Style and Narcissism

Apparently, narcissism gets a chance to flourish quite early in a person due to their askew upbringing. When a child is bestowed with excessive praise or constant criticism by their parents, they're likely to develop narcissistic qualities over time. In most cases, people who are raised with too much love and adoration turn out to be grandiose narcissists, while those who do not receive the affection and support they need become vulnerable narcissists.

Narcissism is a kind of psychological shield that individuals tend to foster within them to combat extreme abuse, criticism, or neglect in their formative years. They feel emotionally wounded because of shame, fear, insecurity, or deprivation they had to suffer as children. So, despite their haughty exteriors, they feel empty, alienated, and have no sense of purpose in life.

Conditional Love by Parents

While love and unceasing acknowledgment are key to a child's growth and self-esteem, they become problematic if shown inconsistently by parents. If a child receives praise for ranking at the top in class, they shouldn't be demeaned for ranking second, third, or fourth. When parents make their child believe that they are supposed to be ahead of others at any cost and that failure is totally unacceptable, they begin to live with the notion that their self-worth is solely based on their achievements. Thus, such a person turns out to be someone who's always after power, beauty, success, and fame. They aren't able to find their true self ever because of the trap of always being the best. They never get a chance to experience disappointments and setbacks in a healthy way. It's like you either want to be the most competent one or you're a total loser. There's no middle ground. So, when a person gets into the habit of feeding their self-esteem with constant praise and admiration (even if it's fake), they stop empathizing with others.

Narcissistic Parents and Their Behavior

A person can also imbibe narcissism unknowingly from their parents. Even if one of the parents has narcissistic traits like being manipulative, full of pride, and insensitive to others, the child is quite likely to model that as they grow up. If a child is reared in an environment where belittling and mocking others is a norm, they're likely to do the same. Parents' behavior, the kind of language they use, the way they treat each other and the people at large, their decisions in different areas, and their life priorities reflect in a child's later life when they become an adult.

Constant Judgment and Comparison

Then there are children who grow up in a family where they're constantly judged and compared with others. One of the two parents (or both) humiliate their children, make them feel inadequate, and stupid whenever they aren't able to meet their expectation in any given scenario (which is quite often). If there are multiple children, they all are pitted against each other. The child who garners all love and adoration today might get totally pulled down tomorrow. No child in such a family receives love in a stable and consistent manner because the parents are angry and irritable most of the time and are unaware of their children's emotional needs. Therefore, when children of such households grow up, they tenaciously try to prove they are more than competent, even though their inner self criticizes them at every step.

Protective Parenting

Parents who are excessively protective of their children may infuse narcissism in them by not allowing them to make their own mistakes and learn from them. There are parents who love their children to such an extent that they simply overlook their bad behavior. Such children begin to believe their wrongdoings are supposed to be their power and they can use it to their advantage whenever they feel like it. On the contrary, authoritative parenting helps a child become a more self-reliant and well-adjusted individual.

Authoritative parenting is a balanced approach to bringing up a child. Such parenting includes being responsive, supportive, and loving along with disciplining a child and setting limits for them. A child is not confused about anything because even their views and curiosity are respected by their parents. If they ask a question, they are given a reasonable answer. The purpose of doing something or not doing something is explained to them so that they learn what's right and what isn't.

Rough Childhood and Narcissism

A child's brain can absorb anything and begin to believe it's true. Since they have nothing to refer to, they take traumatic experiences as their reality, especially if the trauma is caused by their caregivers. According to a study, if you speak to a hundred adolescents, at least 80 of them would have undergone some kind of abuse as children, which led to some kind of psychiatric disorder by the time they turned into an adult.

Not every child is fortunate enough to have a normal, healthy, and a carefree childhood. There are children who get to witness all sorts of unpleasant stuff, such as parents fighting, mothers being abused by alcoholic fathers, living in poverty, undergoing sickness, and many other things. Some children also suffer sexual abuse (which is the worst of all bad experiences) silently for years and years. There's nobody they can confide in about what's been happening with them. Sadly, the abuser is one of the family members. A child who has to face sexual abuse is helpless because they don't know what's happening to them. They feel guilty and ashamed for no fault of their own. They begin to believe that it's happening to them because there's something wrong with them. They're never able to muster up the courage to tell anyone about it because they've no clue what to say. It's a strange situation.

Such children live with this innate belief that they're not good enough and that everybody else is perfect. When they see other children of their age in happy and secure homes being loved by their elders, they feel even worse about themselves. It's like a conviction to them that there's definitely something wrong with them, which is why they're being treated so obnoxiously. When they become an adult with the hidden scars of sexual abuse or any form of abuse for that matter, they develop a very vindictive persona without knowing it. They never really get to know their real selves. The memories of abuse get imprinted on their minds and they keep picturing themselves as someone who isn't attractive, lovable, valuable, or admirable. If they have to face abuse, mistreatment, or manipulation multiple times by different people, they completely lose their trust in people and the idea of receiving love from anyone. They feel everybody out there has an intent to harm them or take advantage of them in some way or the other. So, they become cynical about life and relationships.

Now not everybody like that has to become a narcissist. However, people with unfair and horrifying childhood can develop narcissistic traits, especially a vulnerable kind of narcissism. They're highly likely to be insecure and unhappy in their relationships because of their own negative thinking patterns and controlling behavior. They can turn out to be angry, manipulative, and find it difficult to regulate their emotions. For instance, they might constantly accuse their partners of petty matters and even try to stop them from pursuing their hobbies. They want to be pitiful and want everybody else to be pitiful with them. If they see you happy and enjoying your life, it makes them furious.

Nonetheless, if abuse of any kind is addressed and resolved early on and the child feels supported and heard, it may prevent them from developing any kind of personality disorder.

Narcissism and Major Traumatic Experiences

Some people may turn out to be narcissists due to certain traumatic events or experiences in their early lives. While it's not necessary that everybody who has been through a tragedy or injustice at some point is supposed to become a narcissist, there are narcissists who have traumatic pasts behind them that continue to impact their behavior throughout their lifetime. Prolonged abuse of any kind, bullying by older siblings, unreasonable contempt, and domestic violence may create narcissists. It's hard for certain individuals to regulate their emotions, trust others, and be empathetic because of their negative worldview, which they happen to form over time. The rage and impulsive behavior that they stoop to is the expression of what they endured during the most vulnerable stage of their lives.

So, should you put up with a narcissist who has a traumatic history? Well, you may want to help them by guiding them to seek professional therapy or counseling. However, you're not supposed to take the burden of their poor behavior toward you or others.

Remember, no matter how much trauma a person has been through, it's not an excuse to traumatize others. As an adult, they need to take responsibility for their behavior and actions.

Narcissism and Gender

Is narcissism more prevalent in men than in women? Well, yes. There are reasons behind that, too. Young boys aren't taught to be emotionally aware and show empathy. They're always told to be tough and never cry. Also, as they grow up into men, they're supposed to do really well in their careers, as they're supposed to be providers for their families. Men always have this pressure to own a bigger car, a bigger house, and secure plenty of money because that's what's going to make them feel more powerful and confident in themselves. So, if they tend to be self-absorbed and goal-driven to the degree of even ignoring the emotions and feelings of others, it's not questioned by anyone.

On the other hand, women are expected to be nurturers. They're supposed to take care of their homes, children, parents, and in-laws. They're conditioned to believe that being sacrificial and selfless is a norm, which is why there are fewer women who are narcissists than men. However, it's slowly changing in today's world. Now narcissism is quite commonly seen in women, too. There are women who don't mind being manipulative, self-centered, mean, overbearing, and highly superficial.

So, if both men and women are taught to be aware of their emotions and not be afraid to show them in the right way, they can be saved from turning into narcissists. Parents and elders should be watchful and try to imbibe the right value system in their children right from the start, so that's what they consider as norm and not get carried away by what society teaches them.

Narcissists in Relationships

Narcissists in the interpersonal realm are total losers, while they can be great leaders, music stars, athletes, celebrities, and highly successful entrepreneurs. They know the knack of accumulating wealth but have no idea how to build relationships.

Being in any relationship means connecting with the other person, understanding them, caring for them, and sharing hopes and fears with them. A narcissist, however, isn't able to relate to or fulfill any of these aspects of a relationship because they're too occupied with themselves and their needs. Whether it's a narcissistic parent, partner, or sibling, they simply won't have the ability to love anyone genuinely. They may love others superficially, but not on an emotional level.

Narcissists are incapable of loving others because they don't know how to love themselves in the first place. Yes, they might be self-centered and selfish, but they don't have any real relationship, even with their inner selves, which is why they're enslaved to insecurities, shame, and unknown fears. The only thing they seek from others is a cushion to rest their egos on. If you say anything they don't agree with, they get irritated and angry in a jiffy. It's like you have to walk on eggshells around them. You can either say nice things to a narcissist or stay quiet. If you express your real feelings or confront them about something, it's a threat to them. They don't see you as an individual with your own thoughts, opinions, and perspectives. They just see you as someone who's obligated to meet their needs.

Narcissism is particularly bad for intimate relationships. If you have a narcissistic romantic partner or a parent, it can be quite devastating. You become the source of their narcissistic supply. The relationship can get extremely fatal. While you have the option of leaving a narcissistic spouse, you do have to spend a significant amount of time with narcissistic parents. Here's what to expect:

- A narcissistic parent boasts about their child's achievements in front of others, but never supports them emotionally.
- They constantly remind their child of the things they've done for them and try to make them feel guilty.
- Such parents are mostly absent when their child needs them the most—important life events.
- They make poor excuses to avoid spending time with their children.
- They get angry quite often and keep their child under a lot of pressure.
- They behave selfishly and ruthlessly, and never forgive their child if they find them doing something wrong.

So, when someone is brought up in such an awful parental leadership, they either become highly under-confident and are unable to fight life battles or they replicate their parents' behavior and treat their future partners and children the same way.

A narcissistic brother or sister believes they deserve more recognition and admiration than their other siblings do. Whenever the family gets together, they like to joke about how their physical appearance, talents, smartness, and achievements are better than their younger or older siblings. They often exaggerate their own success to make the other person's success appear smaller. In their heart, they envy you but they act like you're envious of them.

It's normal for a narcissist to disregard your feelings. Even when they seem to show care, they're focused primarily on what's in for them. They make all their decisions based on what's going to suit them without considering other people's will or liking. Also, they may want to control and isolate you. They may not be comfortable with the fact that you have your own set of friends and you want to hang out with them. They may try to cut you off from your social circle and even stop you from pursuing a career of your choice. They may not tell you openly to live according to them, but they will manipulate you into doing what they like. In a matter of time, you may begin to feel like you've lost your identity for the sake of pleasing a narcissist.

The trickiest part of identifying a narcissist is that you're more likely to get attracted to them initially because of their charming ways. It's not so hard to fall in love with a narcissist. However, as time passes, they begin to reveal their real self in different situations. You'll soon realize they aren't exactly who you found appealing in the beginning. Their nastiness will blow your mind, bewilder you, and make you doubt your own self. The sad part is that you end up building a bond with them, which is emotionally and mentally cemented. You feel baffled because you're a normal human being and they expect you to be perfect; if you fail, they make you feel miserable.

NPD Is Hard to Diagnose

Even though NPD is severe and quite common, it's not studied enough. Also, there's very little clinical data available on NPD and interpersonal disabilities, and even if there is any data, the clinicians associated with it have reported having dreadful experiences with NPD patients. There are so many people who are dealing with narcissism in some way or the other, but they aren't aware of it. Most narcissists refuse to come to terms with the idea that there could be a problem with them. They don't want to deal with the shame of confronting their own weaknesses, which is why they refuse to get treated. Most patients have no clue what they are being treated for—they may not agree with the perception of the people who feel victimized by them. In fact, they may feel threatened, blamed, and mistreated by anyone who could be trying to guide them. They may simply disagree with the therapist's interventions and want to put their own opinions at the forefront.

Besides, narcissists can switch to any image type just to fit into a particular situation or to suit a social circle whenever they need to. For instance, a person who's aggressive by nature can project themselves as someone vulnerable and gentle in order to get their needs and wants met. A narcissist can easily gain and maintain control in any given scenario. They can be people-pleasers to be in everyone's good books, but be totally insensitive toward their own family members. So, what appears on the outside can be totally different from reality. Therefore, their narcissistic behavior isn't as obvious as other personality or behavioral issues.

In today's age, almost all of us have some interaction or association with a narcissist, but we don't realize it until we need to deal with them on a deeper level. For example, you may have a narcissistic boss who has been silently harassing you for a while. They may be picking on you for small issues just to make you feel you're not doing your job properly, which might have made you doubt your efficiency and competence. However, their narcissism might not be a problem to them at all. They might be leading a normal life with absolutely no mindfulness of their hurtful attitude. A person's realization and acceptance of their own narcissism is extremely rare.

Also, no matter how much you read and study about narcissism, only a mental health professional can ascertain that somebody has NPD or narcissistic traits. Since narcissism consists of various attitudes and behavior patterns, it's not possible for a layman to diagnose it properly.

Method of NPD Diagnosis

A mental health professional (clinical psychologist or psychotherapist) conducts a one-on-one session with the person and inquires about their medical history. They typically give a questionnaire to the person, which helps to rule out any possibilities of other mental health concerns. They try to focus on how the person thinks, feels, behaves, and communicates with others.

Most mental health professionals go by the DSM-5 model for NPD diagnosis, which comprises the assessment of their:

- personality traits,
- interpersonal relationships,
- professional life,
- self-esteem,

- evolvement of self-image,
- sense of personal identity, and
- capability of being empathetic toward others.

A person needs to have at least five or more of the NPD symptoms to be declared a narcissist officially. However, the most important symptom to consider of narcissism is a lack of empathy for others. The rest of the symptoms can be found in other types of personalities as well, irrespective of whether or not they have a mental disorder. Many of us could be dealing with multiple issues in our lives or be blissfully happy—selfishness, pride, low self-esteem, shame, guilt, and anger—are universal emotions. It's the empathy part that really makes a difference in how a person manages their interactions and relationships. So, we come back to the same point again—narcissism isn't as visible as other disorders because people can pretend to be empathetic. They can show kindness, concern, and be absolutely delightful to be with. However, when it comes to understanding how the other feels and reacts is not a narcissist's domain at all.

While teenagers may have NPD at its developing stage, it's typically diagnosed in adulthood. Since children and adolescents constantly grow (both physically and mentally), it's hard to conclude the kind of personality they're likely to stick with in the long run.

Ironically, narcissism isn't as problematic for someone who actually has it as much as it's for someone who has to deal with it—the person who they're in a relationship with. If you're living with a narcissist, you need to stop feeling responsible for their bad behavior. You need to educate yourself about NPD so that you can handle it better and safeguard your well-being. The next chapter is going to unveil the types of narcissists that exist in the world.

Chapter 2:
Type-Casting the Darkness

You might have met several narcissists and realized that they are all self-centered and lack empathy for others; however, not all narcissists are the same. To be able to deal with them in a better way, you need to know the two distinctive types of narcissists—grandiose and vulnerable. Although both types of narcissists have certain common traits, such as a sense of entitlement, self-obsession, and lack of empathy for others, they are quite different in many ways. While a grandiose narcissist has an elevated self-image, pretentiousness, an exaggerated sense of superiority, arrogance, a tendency to exploit others for their own good, and the hunger for admiration, a vulnerable narcissist is usually defensive, insecure, shame-prone, hypersensitive, full of anger, hostile, lonely, and has low self-esteem.

So, is one better type than the other, or should we state that one is more harmful than the other? Since grandiosity is quite obvious and vulnerability is hidden, the former seems to be more admirable (at least on the surface) than the latter. However, there's more to it. A narcissist with grandiose characteristics is more persistent about being who they are and not bending to accommodate others in any situation. If there's any hope or likelihood of change or improvement, it's with the vulnerable kind of narcissism. A person with vulnerable traits may consider going for therapy and counseling, as their desire to dominate others might not be as intense. However, both types of personalities are problematic in their relationships. Living with a narcissist is unfavorable and unsafe. Thus, it's wise to understand the nuances of their characteristics.

Big Five Personality Traits

Before we understand grandiose and vulnerable narcissism in more detail, let's look at the five-factor model (FFM), which is applicable to almost all kinds of individuals to varying degrees. When a person displays a certain kind of personality consistently, it tends to form self-perceptions, characteristics, values, and influence the expectations of people around them. The big five-factor model can also aid in predicting an individual's response to people in general, and problems and stressful situations of all kinds. Determining the causes and conclusion of narcissistic qualities and NPD are based on many conjoining personality and trait theories.

- Extroversion (aka extraversion)—is a highly sociable and energetic personality trait. Such people usually are super confident, charming, and expressive in their thoughts.
- Neuroticism—is all about sadness and depression. People with high neuroticism tend to get upset easily, worry more, and find it hard to handle stress of any kind.
- Agreeableness—defines a personality type that agrees, cooperates, and helps others. A person who has a high level of agreeableness is empathetic, caring, and always ready to accommodate others.
- Openness—signifies curiosity, interest, and creativity. Such a person is always keen to explore new avenues, try new things, and is open to adventure.
- Conscientiousness—defines someone who's organized, disciplined, detail-oriented, and extremely thoughtful. They never want to be in a situation when they're not prepared for something.

Now, all kinds of narcissists have the above traits (to some degree), except for "agreeableness," because the very essence of narcissism is not agreeing with anybody. A narcissist can be an extrovert, who likes to meet new people, and be opinionated and assertive. However, when these traits are accompanied by pride, selfishness, and insensitivity, we can think of a grandiose kind of narcissist. On the other hand, a person who's an introvert and prefers solitude can be called a vulnerable narcissist if they like to seek attention for who they are and seem to blame the world for their miseries.

A grandiose narcissist is likely to have extraversion, openness, and conscientiousness in them, while a vulnerable narcissist will have more neuroticism. A vulnerable kind of narcissism is low on every other personality trait except for intellect. People with grandiose narcissism tilt toward more socially acceptable and positive qualities, have a high-level of well-being, and are presumably stable. Not so is the case with vulnerable narcissism, as they're socially unfavorable, maladaptive, and mostly depressed. Both types of personalities are difficult to live with even though they are polar opposites. They aren't suitable for relationships because neither of the two kinds have any sensitivity toward the needs of others.

In order to deal with narcissistic personality types, an abused victim needs to understand them deeply. By knowing their abuser's characteristics, the person on the receiving end can prepare themselves mentally for the kind of behavior and relationship they might have in store. With the help of anticipation, their mind and body can get ready for confrontation. The victim will not be shocked to see the bad behavior but will be able to tackle it without stress and even stay safe from future assaults.

Grandiose Narcissism Traits

The first quality to notice about grandiose narcissists is that they overestimate their good qualities, especially their intellectual skills. They're traditionally known for their vanity, arrogance, superficiality, obsession with power, and, of course, grandiosity. They think of themselves as superior to any normal individual who has the quotient of extraversion and openness in them. Since narcissists are so confident in their abilities and intelligence, they naturally feel more powerful than non-narcissists. Grandiose narcissism is a kind of trait that keeps an individual on a high irrespective of who's around them. Such people don't depend on family, friends, or any emotionally close relationship. They may appear to be a loving spouse or a kind friend, but that's just to show the world. There's no real sincerity or devotion toward their loved ones. The sole focus of the relationship is always their own needs and desires. Their dependence on another person is never for emotional reasons. There's clearly no give and take with grandiose narcissists, which is a prerequisite of a normal healthy relationship.

Grandiose Personality Type and Leadership Roles

A grandiose kind of narcissist can be highly suitable for leadership roles because of their highly extroverted personality type. Even if they aren't capable of earning a position or promotion on their own, they still think they're entitled to it. To feel more powerful and secure, extroverts with grandiose traits try to win the favor and goodwill of people who are apparently compliant and non-confrontational. If they don't get praise and acknowledgment from people, they feel hostile about it.

However, many grandiose narcissists do manage to excel as organizational heads and make plenty of money because of their charismatic appeal, boldness, and ability to envision things. For instance, many studies suggest that narcissistic CEOs were more open to making big moves, such as betting on new technology, taking their firms to international markets, and acquiring other companies. Nevertheless, research also indicates that grandiose narcissists can risk the growth of their companies for the sake of their vested interests, which is not a favorable situation.

Since grandiose narcissists tend to be impulsive, overconfident, and unwilling to heed expert advice, they end up making bad decisions most of the time. They don't want to use objectivity before coming to a conclusion because they're so full of themselves.

They believe that if they've chosen something, it has to be good no matter what. Narcissists can be more intuitive than non-narcissists, which isn't wrong. However, even an inkling should be based on some logic and reasoning. Also, they don't value anyone's opinions because they're always doubting others for their knowledge, skills, and understanding. Their heightened sense of superiority and overconfidence keep them from mingling with other people, knowing their perspectives, and being open to unconventional ideas. They can even disregard data and research just to have their way and satiate their own egos.

Blame-Shifting and No Inclination to Learn

Not just that, when they see the wrong outcome, they like to blame others for the same and never care to learn from their failures. On the contrary, if they're successful at something, they like to take all the credit and barely appreciate anybody else for their contribution. Every time they win, they want to use it as an opportunity to showcase their superiority. However, they take losing something as a sign of weakness, which is why they don't want to analyze the reasons for failure and have no inclination for learning. It's hard for them to reconsider and improve their judgment skills.

Grandiose narcissists can also manipulate others for their own benefit. In some scenarios, they can even lie, cheat, and steal to fulfill their own fantasies. They consider themselves to be highly supreme and special, which makes them do all sorts of selfish and thoughtless things.

Vulnerable Narcissism Traits

The other kind of narcissist, which is known as vulnerable, doesn't appear to be an obvious narcissist. In fact, they come across as someone feeble, under-confident, and highly sensitive (which they truly are). They don't have the charm and flamboyance of a grandiose narcissist. In fact, they have no clue about their self-worth, which is why they like to keep to themselves. They try to avoid being in a situation where their flaws are likely to be exposed.

Socially Detached and Extremely Sensitive to Judgment

A vulnerable narcissist is highly sensitive when it comes to emotional hurt. In fact, people need to be extremely careful about saying anything to them. However, they aren't aware of other people's emotions. They don't get the fact that their behavior impacts others and it can be detrimental. Vulnerable narcissists are so engrossed in their anxiety and shame that they fail to notice what's happening around them. They like to be distant from people because they always fear judgment and humiliation of some kind.

Vulnerable narcissism has high levels of neuroticism, which makes such personalities more introverted, pessimistic, and depressed. Since vulnerable narcissists live with this notion that everybody wants to abandon and reject them, they like to isolate themselves in the hope of being accepted by others. They also withdraw socially because they want to avoid interacting with people. Vulnerable narcissists feel if they meet people, they might get ridiculed and harassed for who they are. They tend to experience high emotional volatility, which leads to outbursts of anger and blaming others for the way they feel. They also find it hard to trust others.

Vulnerable narcissists have this inherent insecurity of being criticized, which is why they are difficult to be with. For instance, they may want to be admired by their coworkers at the workplace, but at the same time, they'd have the fear of being hurt. This is because they're psychologically fragile and have entitled expectations from others. So, when they don't get admiration or attention from others (apparently they don't do anything to get that), they feel even more ashamed.

Full of Distrust and Anger

They feel angry because they begin to believe the world is specifically unfair to them. They believe that other people are responsible for anything wrong that has ever happened to them. It's their negative self-evaluation that leads to meaningless incidents in their imaginative world. Vulnerable narcissists weave their own story, play each character on their own, and then later show the ending to the people around them, which leaves everybody clueless and in a state of dismay.

The feelings of extreme pride and deep shame coexist in a vulnerable narcissist, which is why they're hypersensitive to the gentlest of feedback. Narcissists get uncomfortable being laughed at due to their low self-image; however, they don't shy away from mocking others.

Be it their own family members, friends, or any random stranger on the street, everybody finds it stressful to interact with a vulnerable narcissist. However, the narcissist is apparently oblivious to it or they simply choose to deny the fact that their twisted behavior needs correction.

So, whether it's grandiose or vulnerable narcissism, both types of personalities prove to be difficult in all kinds of relationships, especially intimate ones, such as marriage and parental. They show kindness and love with the motive of getting something out of the other person and they resent people they need.

Grandiose vs. Vulnerable Narcissism

According to research and studies, if we discuss agreeableness, vulnerable narcissists usually have a high correlation with the aspect of trust and very little affinity with modesty. On the contrary, grandiose narcissists show a high level of correlation with modesty and a very low level of trust. While both vulnerable and grandiose personalities have antagonistic behavior traits, the urge behind these behavior patterns may not be the same. For example, a vulnerable narcissist may have more hostility in their attitude, while a grandiose narcissist may be more inclined toward self-enhancement (Mahadevan, 2021).

Self-Esteem in the Two Personality Types

In addition, grandiose and vulnerable narcissists display their connection with self-esteem quite differently. A grandiose narcissist typically shows a small to moderate positive affinity, while a vulnerable narcissist depicts a moderate negative correlation with their self-esteem. The disparate connections between the two kinds of narcissist personalities and self-esteem suggest key disparities in the nature of these concepts or hypotheses (Mahadevan, 2021).

Perception of Their Spouses

Besides, people who have any kind of association with either vulnerable or grandiose narcissists also perceive them distinctively. Individuals married to either grandiose or vulnerable narcissists usually find them overbearing, ruthless, intolerant, hypocritical, argumentative, haughty, opportunistic, and demanding. However, people married to grandiose narcissists thought that their spouses were quite in-your-face, astute, presumptuous, assertive, outspoken, and resolute (Mahadevan, 2021).

On the other hand, people married to vulnerable narcissists thought their spouses were emotional, anxious, defensive, bitter, and jittery, and liked to worry and complain quite a lot (Mahadevan, 2021).

Grandiose narcissists come across more as antisocial and people who might have intense personality disorders (PDs), while on the contrary, vulnerable narcissists seem to be closer to detached and borderline PDs. Interestingly, if we consider the shared inclinations to negative emotions, vulnerable narcissists are more likely to have borderline personality disorder (BPD) than NPD.

Additionally, these findings suggest that vulnerable narcissists, just like people who have BPD, do not think about self-injury or attempt suicide (Mahadevan, 2021).

Behavior Patterns in Social Scenarios

It's possible to identify and distinguish the two categories of narcissists by their attitude and behavior in a social setting. A grandiose narcissist has superior social skills. They can be quite magnetic and charming with the way they speak and act in a crowd. Not so is the case with a vulnerable narcissist, as they have poor social skills. They may not attract many people because of their shyness and anxiety in social scenarios. Another big difference between the two personality types is that grandiose narcissists are enterprising, candid, and decisive about chasing their goals in order to take their success to the next level, while vulnerable narcissists aren't as courageous and determined. In fact, they're more self-protective and all they want to do is try to reduce the degree of failure (Mahadevan, 2021).

Inclination Toward Social Status and Inclusion

According to a couple of studies, researchers tried to assess the levels of the two main types of narcissism in 676 adults living in the United States. They also reviewed the intensity of their desire to achieve a certain status and inclusion in society, along with finding out to what extent they thought they had accomplished their goals (Mahadevan, 2021).

The result indicated that both grandiose and vulnerable narcissists wanted a certain social status quite intensely. The only difference was that grandiose narcissists thought they had attained the social position they were looking for, while vulnerable narcissists thought they did not achieve the social standing they deserved and felt entitled to (Mahadevan, 2021).

Not just that, grandiose narcissists didn't really obtain social inclusion, and nor did they care for it much. Vulnerable narcissists, on the other hand, did care a lot for social inclusion, but they did not get it. So, grandiose narcissists seemed to be content with the idea that they had accomplished their social aspirations, but the personality type of vulnerable narcissism did not (Mahadevan, 2021).

Both grandiose and vulnerable narcissists seek respect and adulation from others. However, it's only a grandiose kind of a narcissist who manages to be in the spotlight and bask in their glory. The vulnerable kind of a narcissist usually remains on the sidelines, not knowing what to do and waits for others to honor them for no reason. They resentfully seek praise and admiration but fail because of their timidity and pessimism (Mahadevan, 2021).

Other Narcissistic Personality Styles

There are many other types of narcissists that exist. Most of them may not be noticeably narcissists, which is why the people they interact with have no clue how they're being influenced. These personalities may not have NPD, but can have certain narcissistic traits that may not be conducive to relationships of any kind.

It's important to know them, as each type can be dangerous in their own ways.

Covert Narcissism vs Overt Narcissism

Most people think vulnerable and covert narcissism are interchangeable. But they're not. Just like grandiose and vulnerable are opposites in the way they manifest their narcissism, covert and overt are also two sides of the same coin. A grandiose narcissist can be overt or covert—they can be obviously pretentious and cocky or they can be entitled and seek validation in a suppressed way. On the other hand, a vulnerable narcissist can also either show their pessimism, anger, and hostility in an overt manner or keep it hidden—which is why we call it covert. So, both grandiose and vulnerable narcissists can be either overt or covert.

Covert narcissists also think highly of themselves, but in a secret way. They're passive-aggressive. They come across as depressive because of the so-called self-pity that they exude. For instance, they may say, "I could have been a great artist only if somebody would have given me a chance." They feel the world hasn't given them a fair chance to become who they wanted to be. They don't even take constructive feedback in the right way. They're so hypersensitive to criticism.

A person who's depressed but is not a narcissist will not blame the world for not being able to accomplish something. They may say things like, "I just wasn't good enough or maybe I should give it another try." However, the covert narcissist never takes ownership of what they did wrong.

Malignant Narcissism

Malignant narcissists are typically all the things that a grandiose narcissist is, but they're also really mean. They're more exploitative, manipulative, coercive, and deceitful than other kinds of narcissists. They do all kinds of bad things like stealing money, cheating on their partners, lying, and they even engage in criminal behavior. They're almost psychopathic. They can do anything to be in power and control others. They often put their own pleasure above other people's concerns.

Also, they tend to accuse others (spouses, friends, employees, or business associates) of unethical behavior that they engage in— they presume if they can do wrong things, others must also be doing the same. They're also more vindictive than other narcissistic types. So yes, malignant narcissists can be the most dangerous of all kinds of narcissistic personality types.

Communal Narcissism

Communal narcissists seek validation for their "good" works. They like to propagate about all the rescue missions they carry out and all the charity they do. They want the world to know about their generosity and be applauded for it. They don't do good things quietly. Also, they're hypocritical in their approach to doing good. They might not do what they suggest to others. For instance, they may tell you, "Oh, you should be more passionate about community causes." However, they won't do enough themselves. They do less work but showcase it flamboyantly to the world. They're also harshly judgmental toward people who don't say or do the same things as they do. For example, if they've turned into a vegan, they're going to criticize those who eat meat.

It can be highly frustrating to deal with such personalities because they won't allow you to have your say in any of the matters. They're control freaks like all narcissists.

Benign Narcissism

Benign narcissists are the most tolerable of all the other types of narcissists because they aren't really harmful per se. While benign narcissists are full of themselves, extroverted, and entitled just like the grandiose kind of narcissists, they don't abuse people in a damaging way. They're self-obsessed, haughty, shallow, and immature. They like to talk about themselves and brag about everything that they own. They're excellent at social skills and can invigorate a party with their presence. However, when it comes to developing a deep emotional relationship with someone, they're totally clueless.

Even when they age and become parents of older children, benign narcissists still remain quite childish and frivolous in their ways. They aren't able to manage serious stuff like raising kids, understanding their needs, and taking responsibility. So, it can be quite challenging for their partners to handle their superficiality and immaturity all the time.

Neglectful Narcissism

Neglectful narcissists are different from other kinds of narcissists in quite a few ways, such as they're not so blatant about validation seeking or boasting about their greatness. They might not even abuse you verbally or physically. However, they can be extremely difficult people to be with, especially for those who share an intimate relationship with them. As the name suggests, a neglectful narcissist ignores you, makes you feel your existence doesn't matter to them, and they don't care how you feel about it. They aren't concerned about anything related to you—your job, personal interests, or your well-being. They like to be detached from human emotions most of the time and wouldn't want to engage in any sort of discussion or conversation unless they want something from you.

It's extremely hurtful and lonely to be with someone like that long term because they live in their own world and like to do their kind of stuff without you. They may be workaholics, social workers, or volunteers at church; however, they won't spend any time with people who're their immediate family. It gets more painful when they spend time with their coworkers or catch up with their college friends, but never even acknowledge your presence when they see you. Their behavior emanates from their belief that they're above you and that they don't need to be attached to you. They don't value their loved ones because they feel powerful and confident by making money, being successful, and doing whatever motivates them.

All kinds of narcissists believe they're the most important people and that it's not their responsibility to take care of anybody else in terms of how other people feel or think. Narcissists don't know how to reciprocate in relationships. They only know how to take and fulfill their own needs. They want to "win" at any cost because losing to them is a failure, and that is a threat to them.

By knowing characteristic traits of the different types of narcissistic personalities, you can identify them more easily and avoid starting a friendship or any form of relationship with them, and if you think you already have one of the narcissistic types in your family—maybe a parent, young child, spouse, boyfriend or a girlfriend, you can learn how to cope with their behavior (which you'll read about ahead in the book) so that you're able to preserve your well-being and not live antagonized by the pain.

Chapter 3:
To Battle—Manipulation You Need to Recognize

Narcissists need to feel powerful all the time. It's their way to console their fragile egos. They make you feel special only to gain control over you. Once you give into their manipulative ways, they gain power over you. They like to play mental games with you so that you surrender to their whims and fancies. It's imperative to know these techniques as they use them very cleverly to control you. Sadly, when it's an interpersonal relationship, you receive no outside support or understanding. Sometimes, people don't even believe you. Therefore, the more you know your predator and their game plan, the better shielded you can be.

Be aware that you can be manipulated in a relationship and you won't even know until it makes you uncomfortable and miserable. If you think something is not right, think of ways to tackle it, get help, or make an exit plan (more on this in chapter 5). Begin by learning about narcissistic behavior and traits. You must try to understand the "why" behind their desire to manipulate people around them to be able to deal with their psychology. If you don't allow them to control you, they feel threatened and tend to react in anger. It's like they feel a loss of power, which is totally unacceptable to them. So, they may attack you verbally, emotionally, or even physically to vent out their frustration.

Manipulation Tactics Used by Narcissists

To keep yourself sane and not be affected by a narcissist's behavior, you must know their manipulation strategies:

- Narcissists typically make the codependents their scapegoats for their manipulation. They take advantage of the other person's weaknesses and hold them responsible for whatever goes wrong in the relationship. The codependent constantly feels confused and guilty because their sense of self is distorted by their narcissistic partner.
- They win your heart pronto by making you feel on top of the world as soon as they meet you. Don't be surprised if they tell you that they haven't met a person like you and that they hold you very special. That's exactly their way of making you knuckle under their will. Their charm is deceptive and short-lived. Once you build a bond with them, they begin to misbehave and treat you nastily.
- They maintain control over you by drawing out emotions like shock and guilt from time to time. If you do anything to disappoint your narcissistic partner, spouse, or friend, be ready to receive a dramatic reaction. After which, you'll try your level best to avoid messing up with them.
- They simply deny their own words to weaken and trick you for their own gain, which is known as gaslighting.
- They may use flattery sometimes to make you do what they want and then again turn to being aggressive the next day. The switch can be overlapping, which can be quite confusing for the victim.

Dark Psychology Manipulative Ways of Narcissists

Remember, narcissists devise many control tactics to stay in power and suck your sense of self-worth out of you. They want to drain your energy out and destabilize your emotional health. If you don't know their tactics, they're going to succeed in hurting, demeaning, and exploiting you.

Blame Shifting

This can be better termed as projection, which we all use to shake off accountability of our own faults on somebody else and feel safe. Narcissists like to do it all the time because they're excessively ashamed of their short-comings. They're just too scared to expose their flaws to the world, which is why they conveniently like to shift the blame for any wrong outcome on whoever they find most gullible. If you're in a close relationship with them, you're bound to get trapped in their blame shifting scheme. For instance, if they're not productive enough at work, they're likely to accuse their manager of being inefficient.

Lying or Withholding Truth

Hiding the truth or making false statements is also one of their ways to have control over a relationship. They like to keep you unaware of certain things about them so that they can use it against you whenever they need to. They don't have the guts to keep the association with anyone transparent and truthful. Lying is their tool to stay afloat on the waves of self-pride.

Deviating Arguments

If you happen to argue with a narcissist, you're in for some real trouble, as they're never going to stick to the main point of the subject. They may say something totally absurd and will expect you to agree with them. You've no right to disagree with them, no matter how logical or clear your point is. They're most likely to attack you in every area of your life—from your past to your present and to everything you do. They're going to talk about everything under the sun just to prove you wrong.

However, you should avoid arguing with a narcissist for your own good. As soon as you sense a meaningless discussion, you should immediately turn around and engage in something more fruitful.

Making Hurtful Comments

A manipulator knows the things that may upset you or make you feel hurt, and they deliberately attack you, exactly there, with their words. They like to make comments to pull you down; however, they never admit to the fact that they had hurtful intentions. They believe it's their right to say anything to you, which is also one of their ways to feel powerful.

Making Blanket Statements

They fail to understand the depth and varied aspects of a conversation but like to generalize everything based on their black and white thinking. They simply overlook the nuances of a topic and the different perspectives that can emerge from it. Thus, talking to a narcissist about anything is a frustrating experience.

Discouraging and Criticizing

They're never happy with your attempts to do anything new or creative. If you want to join a dance class, start a new hobby, or venture into a business, they have all the negative points to offer. They have no constructive feedback to share, but only discouragement to push your way to stop you from doing what you want to do.

Distorting Your Thinking and Feelings

Toxic people presume to know your thoughts, feelings, and emotions. If you say something to them, they like to put words in your mouth based on their own delusions. For instance, if you tell them you need time to decide on a matter, they might say, "Oh, so you need time to think whether you want to spend time with me or not." They have no intent to understand your true thought process and willingness. All they're focused on is their own fallacies and they are totally unapologetic about it.

Devaluing Your Opinions and Concerns

If you try to express your pain, ideas, or opinions with a toxic person, they like to ignore it. They might roll their eyes, smile smugly, or scoff in response to your grievances. Their goal is to make you feel devalued, dismissed, and unheard. They don't have the courage to face anything unpleasant or complex, so they simply disregard what you say. They simply don't have the ability to soothe your pain or comfort you because of their callous heart.

Monitoring and Stalking

Manipulators like to keep an eye on everything you do, and everywhere you go. They don't even shy away from checking your laptop, phone, and your personal notes to find out what's going on with you. By doing so, they want to be sure that you're under their control and aren't doing anything to upset them. For instance, if you decide to learn a new language and enroll yourself in the same, they may tell you not to do it. They may say, "Why do you need to do it? Do you have plans to move to a new country?"

It's always hard for them to let you make your independent decisions, which is why they monitor you so that they can stop you from doing anything that might not suit them.

Intruding in Your Personal Space

Sometimes it can be quite obvious while sometimes it can be subtle; the invasion of your privacy is your manipulator's birthright. They can cross boundaries without apology, interrupt when you're talking to somebody, and try to manage your decisions on your behalf. They can say anything in front of anyone without any consciousness of how it's going to impact you. The idea behind such behavior is to keep you from making positive changes in your life and gaining anyone's support.

Threatening You if You Disagree With Them

Narcissists, whether covert or overt, aren't able to handle disagreement at all. If you don't match their unreasonable standards or ideals, you're good for nothing. They try to threaten you, overtly or covertly, to make you do what they want. They may say, "If you go out shopping with your sister, I'm not coming with you for the doctor's appointment tomorrow."

However, you don't have to submit to their wishes. You should deal with their threats head on by either making your point clear or seeking external support.

Highlighting Your Failures and Diminishing Your Successes

Your narcissistic abuser will always try to pick on you to make you feel like a failure while keeping your successes under wraps. They ensure that your achievements aren't talked about much because they want to be the only one to be praised and applauded. For example, if you've won a contest that's really valuable to you, they might just say, "Oh, nice! Well, congratulations!" But they won't magnify it and encourage you to continue to pursue what you like and keep winning. On the contrary, they'll make sure to remind you of instances where you fell short and say things like, "You couldn't get promoted at work because you're competent enough."

Their self-absorbed character makes them live with this constant fear of being overshadowed if they let anyone receive their due praise.

Sabotaging Your Life Goals and Happiness

Since narcissists want you to be solely focused on them and their needs, they try to destroy everything else that makes you happy and fulfilled. Be it your other relationships (parents, siblings, and friends), life goals, dreams, or any pursuit that makes you come alive, your abuser ensures that you don't go after any of those things because they fear losing control over your emotions and feelings. They think that by letting you do whatever makes you happy or allowing you to spend time with your loved ones, your focus will shift from them to other people and things that are also important to you.

Playing With Your Insecurities

Your abuser may not always appear to be blatant about their snide remarks and accusations. They may provoke you innocently sometimes. They like to drive you into a mindless conversation with the idea of hitting on your weakest spot, emotionally. They like to talk about topics that take you back to your wounds. In a little while, they may say, "I hope I didn't hurt you." That's their fake concern for your emotions. Their real purpose is to tear you down. So, you should step away as soon as you sense a situation like that.

Blackmailing Emotionally

Your abuser is aware of your emotional needs, such as love, affection, and approval, which they use against you whenever they need to. They blackmail you emotionally if you don't adhere to their demands. They threaten you about withdrawing support if you don't do what they want or go against their wishes. This is their tactic to make you feel obligated to do whatever they want and be sorry if you don't.

Making You Feel Guilty

Your abuser doesn't hesitate to tell you that you don't care enough or you're just too selfish. They may also tell you that you have more than you deserve and that you don't value anything. They may completely disregard what you do and how diligently you take care of them. By doing so, they want to make you doubt your own self, feel guilty, be anxious, and have no voice of your own.

Creating Fake Situations to Draw Attention

Manipulators also intentionally push you toward trouble just to be able to rescue you. They create situations where you'd need their help so that they can always be in a dominant position. It's their trick to make you want to trust them and eventually depend on them. Once you completely believe them, they begin to reveal their cruel ways.

Twisting or Denying Facts

Abusers simply refuse to stick to their own words and statements. They like to twist and even deny saying and doing something in the past, making you doubt your own sanity, memory, and perception. They may completely turn away from their own opinions just to suit the present circumstances and avoid taking any accountability.

Rationalizing Their Bad Behavior

Narcissists always have some excuse for their bad behavior. They may try to make sense out of nonsense just to prove their point right. They're more likely to do so behind your back in the company of other people who might not be aware of the undertone of manipulation. The intent is to make you come across as someone dumb, immature, and too hard to get along with. They tend to project you as someone who overreacts to situations and often misunderstands while they're always reasonable and accommodating in any given scenario.

Making You Feel Like a Child

Manipulators often try to make you feel as if you have no understanding of life matters and lack the ability to make wise decisions and choices. They do it to change your own opinion about yourself and shatter your self-belief. This is also due to their own lack of confidence and hidden insecurities. Thus, you shouldn't take it personally. Whenever there's an opportunity to make a decision, be confident about it and go with what you think is right.

Harassing You for Your Failures

Narcissists either glorify or completely write you off for who you are. Such a situation is quite common in families and households where there are children who are different from each other. If one is a topper in class and excels at everything, they're given special treatment and made to feel superior to others. However, the one who isn't able to do as well in studies and other activities is treated like a loser and somebody that deserves only criticism.

Finding Fault With Whatever You Do

To a narcissist, you can never do anything right. It's like you're damned if you try to do something that may suit them and damned if you don't. It's their way of psychologically defeating you and making you doubt your own judgment. You'll keep wondering and thinking, "What is wrong with me? Why am I unable to do anything right?" Such futile thoughts begin to erode your self-esteem. Thus, you shouldn't get in the trap of their mental games and be firm about your own way of doing things.

Playing Victim

Instead of owning their own nastiness, a manipulator tries to portray themselves as a victim of any given circumstance. They try to justify that if they behaved in a certain way, it's because of someone else's behavior and that it was the best way to tackle the situation. Such manipulation aims at evoking compassion and pity from the other person in order to dismiss the blame.

Abusing You Even More as You Go back to Them

A narcissist abuses their victim, even more, when they're given a second chance. They don't react to kindness and empathy, but only to consequences. The more you allow them to mistreat you, the worse they will get. Therefore, it's never wise to return to your abuser ever, no matter how sorry they are for their behavior. In fact, going back to them gives them a signal that you can't do without them and they can win you back anytime.

Getting Intimate Too Soon

A narcissist is always quick to start a romantic relationship and gives an impression that they're okay talking about their deep desires, insecurities, and vulnerabilities. They do it to have their partner reciprocate in the same manner. However, when they do, the narcissist keeps a record of it only to misuse it against them whenever the opportunity arises. They're quick to propose, quick to discuss a dreamy future, and quick to make you fall in love with them.

Giving You Silent Treatment

People who're self-absorbed and toxic like to punish their loved ones by giving them silent treatment once in a while. They like to stop talking to you, leave the house for hours, and even days sometimes making you wonder what has gone wrong. As a result, you may want to avoid certain topics of discussion, conceal certain emotions that may possibly upset your abuser, and try to behave to accommodate them.

Taking All Financial Reins in Their Hands

A narcissistic person may make all kinds of bad financial decisions and allow you no part to play whatsoever. They like to hide their finances from you. However, if anything goes wrong, you're declared the culprit. They even stop you from earning your own money, so that you're always dependent on them for all your needs. They make their own spending decisions without your intervention, but if you choose to spend money, it has to be aligned with their priorities.

Controlling You Persuasively

Sometimes a narcissist may just control you in a compelling way and not necessarily get aggressive. For instance, they may tell you, "Why don't you quit your job? It's not good for you. I make enough to sustain the two of us." They try to play with your mind tactfully rather than telling you something without mincing words.

If you can relate to the above points (or at least a few of them), it's time you break the chain of abuse and set yourself free. The first step is to be aware of dark psychology manipulation. So, watch out for the signs and once you know you're being manipulated, take effective action to end it before you lose your sense of individuality and self-respect. Remember, your abuser will skip no chance to cross relationship boundaries and denigrate you. So, it's your responsibility to set certain boundaries and make sure they're never broken. If you feel emotionally, physically, or verbally abused in a relationship, seek support as soon as possible. Sometimes, the abuse or manipulation can be so subtle that you may not be able to discuss it with anyone. Even your friends and family may find it hard to understand you. However, you still have to stand your ground and do what is right and fair.

Self-Defense Tactics You Can Use to Deal With a Narcissist

If you've no choice but to deal with a narcissist, it's important that you stop them from abusing you and learn how to take charge of your life again. It may sound hard, but it isn't as long as you're determined to protect your identity and self-respect. You need to stop being submissive and tolerant of any unfair treatment. In order to cope with someone's narcissism, you need to pay attention to their daily behaviors and understand their thinking patterns. Whether it's a situation where you've decided to divorce a narcissist or you're staying with a narcissistic parent, knowing their behavior patterns can help you prepare yourself mentally, stay away from their weird attitude, and set certain boundaries. In a case of separation or divorce, you can mitigate stress and continue to rear your children without being in touch with your ex-spouse. You can also keep your mental well-being in good shape.

By applying the below mentioned strategies, you can make your relationship with a narcissist a little more harmonious and less exhausting:

Stick to the Facts

The best way to shut up a narcissist's lies is to give them the facts. They're not going to skip any chance to gaslight you and try to make you believe that you're in the wrong. They can go to any length to prove that you're at fault and that you should be sorry. They can deny a blatant truth, twist statements, and play the victim. So, don't let them pull you into their game. You should always keep a record of your conversations or transactions with them—messages, emails, phone calls, bank statements, and other documents. By sticking to facts, you'll be able to safeguard yourself from their manipulative ways.

Replace "I" or "You" With "We"

Since a narcissist can never be wrong and they don't care about your opinion or perspective, you shouldn't exhaust yourself arguing with them. The smarter tactic would be to use the word "we" and kick out "I" or "you" from your sentences. When you say "we," it can alleviate heated arguments and fights and you can possibly reach a solution with them. You can overshadow them in a war of words by making statements like, "We need to address this issue, which is more important than anything else right now," or "We shouldn't mock or blame each other for petty issues. We can resolve this together."

Choose Not to React to Their Tactics

Reacting to a narcissist's snide comments and gaslighting remarks can be your biggest mistake. Remember, they want to infuriate you and make you feel frustrated and anxious. So, don't give them what they want. Instead, move away from them and speak out a few positive things about yourself to keep your sanity and self-esteem safe. As soon as you hear them lash out at you, tell yourself they're insecure, full of hidden shame, and need help. Never take their nasty comments and criticisms seriously. You should pity them for behaving inappropriately and stop feeling sorry for yourself. If you find it too hard to handle and can't control your anger, try deep breathing and start imagining yourself in a beautiful place.

Use the ABC Technique

Now here's a communication technique you can use to control the narcissist in your life and make them interact with you more respectfully. It's called the ABC technique, in which A stands for 'affect,' which means your feelings. So, when you make 'affect' or feeling statements, make use of "I," such as "I'm feeling scared, uncomfortable, or sad." However, your choice of words should depend on the kind of relationship you share with the narcissist. You should refrain from using strong words like sad or scared with someone you share an impersonal relationship with (e.g. coworker). It's better to use your discretion here. The idea is to let the other person know your specific experience. Make sure you don't use "you" when you're expressing your feelings.

B stands for 'behavior,' which means the interaction or action that instigated your feelings. So, to communicate that, you can say things like, "When you make sarcastic remarks," "When I get to hear only negative things about me," or "When you don't let me complete my sentences."

C stands for 'correction,' which means the change you expect from the narcissist. Remember, when you want to show assertiveness, it should always be garbed with politeness and should sound like a request and not a command. Consider it a kind of coaching, where you want to tell the other person how they can work on their interpersonal skills. You may say things like, "Can you stop yelling at me?" "Can you tell me how you'd like to take this forward?" or "Can you be polite?"

Never Doubt Yourself

Keep in mind, you need to trust yourself and never fall for self-doubt with a narcissist. They will often make you think that you didn't get things straight and that there's a problem with your memory. They lie to be able to prove themselves right all the time. So, you need to be vigilant about their game plan and be firm about your own understanding and ideas about whatever situation you're in.

Ignore Their Behavior

The best way to maintain your calm and not get into a frustrating situation with a narcissist is to ignore their bad behavior or false claims. If you try to confront them or try to teach them a lesson, it's going to be futile. They're good at excruciating you mentally and emotionally by dragging you into long and tiring arguments (often monologues) and showing you their outrage just to scare you off. They're most likely to blame you for everything and try to act as if they did nothing wrong at all. So, the wise thing to do would be to nullify their toxic behaviors by simply ignoring them.

Set Boundaries

Let your abuser know what you do not like in their behaviors and won't tolerate at any cost. Also, warn them of the consequences if they continue to disrespect you. Try to sound assertive when you lay down your boundaries and make sure to take action if they are broken. They should know you have a mind of your own and it's not so easy to mess with you. When you set boundaries in a relationship, you get your power back. For example, you may state, "If you ridicule me or use curse words, I'm not going to talk to you anymore," "If you snoop into my phone in my absence, I'm not going to share anything with you," or "If you yell at me, I'm not going to engage in any conversation with you."

The more particular and consistent you're with your boundaries and the consequences, the better control you can have on your narcissistic partner (or whoever you need to deal with) and their nasty behavior.

Avoid Arguments or Handle Them Smartly

It's almost impossible to win arguments with a narcissist, so you should try and avoid them as much as possible for your own peace and mental well-being. If in case, there's something that you really need to address, make sure you do it tactfully. For instance, if they try to distort your statements and try to escalate the matter, reinstate your original words and keep repeating them. Never make the mistake of defending yourself or responding to their twisted understanding.

People who spend many years being humiliated by their significant others find it even harder to escape the hell they've been part of. They almost feel their pain is irreparable. However, all kinds of pain are curable. If you've been in a manipulative relationship for years, you can reinstate your being. You can become the person that you always wanted to be. You need to be brave, believe in yourself, and find the right kind of support system. Most importantly, you need to bid adieu to your abuser forever and never give them another chance. You've spent enough years living for them with only frustration, anger, self-doubt, and resentment in return. Now is your time to lighten up and live for yourself unabashedly.

Chapter 4:
The Gaze—Why a Narcissist Pays Attention

Your body language plays a key role in defining your interpersonal skills. It's not just your spoken words, but also your facial expressions and body stance that send signals that the narcissist picks up on. They break you down with manipulation and then read your body language with the end goal of owning you. If you appear to be submissive and vulnerable, they tend to take advantage of that and try to dominate you. Hunched shoulders, a fearful and sad expression on the face, and a submissive body posture can indicate a body language that is agreeable and compliant, which means the person can be manipulated easily. While there's nothing wrong in being a certain way, your body language shouldn't make other people get a vibe that your will and emotions can be sabotaged.

While a genuinely kind, generous, and considerate person (who's also confident and comfortable in their own skin) may not treat you unfairly because of your feeble body language, a narcissist will definitely attempt to make you their scapegoat for their own good. Narcissists feed on frail personalities. Their inner shame, insecurities, and lack of self-esteem compel them to act dominant with people who happen to be polite and meek, mistaking them to be weak. The more patience and endurance you show to narcissistic manipulators, the worse they behave with you. They see your "undefended" body language and prey on you.

Narcissists pick and choose their victims based on what they see and gauge. If they see someone with a confident and authoritative body stance—someone who maintains glaring eye contact, they're less likely to mess with such a person. While it's not a rule, they typically like to ensnare people who exude indecisiveness and vulnerability. For instance, if you're at a restaurant with a bunch of friends and are looking around to see what others are ordering, it gives a narcissist a clue that you seek approval for your choices.

Since narcissists have a secret agenda behind everything they do, you should be careful and not fall for their "fake" authenticity. For instance, if you realize you're being wooed by someone domineering, you can give them an icy glare to smash their hopes down. They're likely to lose interest, sensing you aren't really timid.

Recognize a Potential Narcissist by Their Body Language

To keep narcissists at bay, you need to know about their body language and how they project themselves in public. Watch out if you happen to notice the following in a person:

- An overt narcissist is likely to have pride and arrogance in their postures. A narcissistic man usually likes to walk with open shoulders and a flamboyant stride, while a narcissistic woman may enter a room like a beauty pageant winner. Whether it's male or female, a narcissist gives off only one message through their body movements, which is— "There's nobody better than me. I deserve all the compliments, admiration, and attention."
- Narcissists never smile when they meet somebody, or the better way to put it is that they lack the gleam in their eyes when they faintly try to smile. They usually remain expressionless when they greet a person (unless they want something from the other person). Also, there's no excitement or happiness in their voice or style of talking.

- The fact that a narcissist has emotionless body language is because they aren't aware of many emotions. They don't feel different the emotions that any normal person feels. The only emotions they know are happiness, sadness, fear, envy, jealousy, guilt, and shame, which they depict through their postures and expressions. Of course, they express their guilt and shame by showing bursts of anger and demeaning others.
- They can completely disregard somebody's presence and act as if the other person doesn't even exist—it's their way of feeling superior.
- A narcissist is always looking out for their victim. They stare at others with dead eyes. They pay close attention to other people's body language and the signals they give off.
- Some narcissists can even touch others in a manner that doesn't feel right. It can be sexual or dominant. However, they get extremely upset if it's done to them by someone else.
- They also like to push people away and be in front for the sake of being noticed by eminent people. They do this to ensure that nobody else is even able to start a conversation with someone they want to mingle with.
- They generally like to break queues and brush people aside to have their way, even when there's no emergency or any genuine concern they need to deal with.

The above examples of body language can help you stay on your toes and show restraint in giving in to the advances of a potential narcissist.

Significance of Body Language

Why is body language so important in our interpersonal relationships and why should you bother to improve it? Each person has their own language that isn't just limited to words and phrases. As individuals, we have different roles to play in our day-to-day lives, personally, professionally, and socially, which we fulfill with the help of how we express ourselves through the language of body mannerisms.

Body language is a person's physical behavior, expressions, and movements to communicate nonverbally, which is mostly instinctive and not really thought out. A person can convey their feelings and intent through their facial expressions, postures, hand gestures, eye contact, and voice tone. If they want to be kind and helpful to somebody, they'll have a pleasant body language to indicate the same. However, if they want to be rude and disinterested, they will garb sternness.

You can make people feel comfortable, make them want to be around you, and build trust with the way you use your body language. On the other hand, you can also confuse, offend, and intimidate others with your nonverbal communication. So, the way you conduct your body language affects your interaction and relationships with other people. If you want to have solid connections with others, you need to have warmth and friendliness in your body language.

Also, you should be able to match your words with your body language for effective communication and relationship building. For instance, if your spoken words indicate that you want to help somebody, your facial expressions shouldn't show your disagreement. Remember, body language is a natural form of communication. It's going to reveal the truth about what you're actually thinking and what you intend to do. If your words and body language contradict, people you interact with will get a sense that you're being dishonest, which is why reading people's physical gestures can be a good way of judging them.

Types of Body Language and Their Messages

There isn't just one way to communicate with your body language. A person can express and make a point in so many different ways.

Body Posture and Movement

People get a sense of who you are by the way you stand, walk, sit, or hold your head and shoulders. Your body movement and carriage can give people signals about what you intend to do and how confident you are. Even your subtle mannerisms make people notice you and form an opinion about you.

When you're in a new setting, surrounded by strangers, try to hold your aplomb and no-nonsense attitude. Let your postures and movements radiate sternness for other people to get a sense of your strength and headstrong personality. Even if you're not so, give them an impression of being so.

Facial Expressions

From positive emotions like happiness, excitement, anticipation, and satisfaction to negative emotions like sadness, anxiety, fear, envy, and disgust, a human face is capable of expressing so many different feelings. So, if you're smiling, it can indicate you want to welcome somebody, are happy to have them at your place, or like talking to them.

If you're with someone who seems to be a narcissist, try managing your facial expressions and give them a vibe that you aren't interested in their game plan.

Eye Contact

Perhaps the strongest way to connect with another person is by looking into their eyes. You can't be interested in a person and look away. Making eye contact with someone you're talking to gives them an assurance that you're listening to them intently. It also goes to show that you like the person and want to continue the conversation with them. Of course, you shouldn't stare into someone's eyes relentlessly to make them uncomfortable.

Hand Gestures

We all use some kind of hand gesture every day to convey certain messages to different people that we come across on a personal and professional level. We wave goodbyes, beckon, point at something with our fingers, and use many hand gestures while trying to make a point in a conversation. However, certain hand gestures like the "OK" sign aren't taken as something positive in some nations. So, you need to be careful about how you use your hand movements if you're in a new country.

Make sure you don't use your hand gestures in a timid manner, inviting the narcissist to presume you're their soft target. For example, refrain from hiding your hands under the table while talking. In fact, you should use your hands appropriately to show power and wisdom.

Touch and Space

While it's inappropriate to touch anybody you're not too familiar with, a touch can mean a lot of things in a nice and pleasant way to the other person. For example, if you extend your hand for a warm handshake or a pat on somebody's back to encourage them, it can be quite helpful. But there are people who hold your arm too tightly to show control or tap on your head in a patronizing manner, which can be an alarming cue to warn you to stay away!

Also, standing too close to somebody in a social setting is not right. Invading someone's space is utterly disgraceful. Each person deserves their own physical space, which can differ based on the relationship shared with another person, the kind of situation they're in, and their culture.

Tone of Voice

Your voice tone is the oil of your message. It's like how you say something determines the outcome of what you say. When people hear you speak, they don't just hear your words but notice your voice, rate of speech, volume, and inflection as well. Your tone of voice can make another person feel a certain way depending on the emotion (sarcasm, anger, humor, or affection) you exude.

So, if you're chatting with an overconfident person (possibly a narcissist) at a party, try to keep your voice assertive. This will ensure that whatever you say is heard and not taken for granted.

Improving Your Nonverbal Communication

The more aware you're of your body language, the better you can deal with a narcissist. You need to focus on each experience that you're part of, which means you should try to be fully conscious of the present moment so that you can put your best foot forward in terms of attention, responses, and communication. For instance, if you're talking to somebody, make sure you're listening to what they're saying and paying attention to their nonverbal cues. You shouldn't be checking your messages on the phone or be thinking about the kind of day you anticipate at work. You can achieve that by being aware of your emotions and managing your stress.

Being Aware of Your Emotions

You may feel a variety of emotions from time to time, but you might not acknowledge them, which isn't healthy. You should know your emotions and how they impact you. You don't have to be guilty of feeling a certain emotion, nor should you suppress it. There are ways to channel your emotions so that they don't harm you or others. If you don't recognize your own emotions, you won't be able to send appropriate silent cues to other people. You should also be able to gauge other people's emotions and feelings behind their nonverbal language. This will help you connect with them better, and establish trust, care, and understanding in the relationship.

If you stay disconnected from your true emotions, you're likely to behave weirdly and may end up hurting people because no matter what you say, your behavior won't comply with that. When you learn to tackle emotions like sadness, fear, and anger, you can manage your physical behavior more effectively and communicate better.

Managing Stress

If you feel stressed about something or maybe you don't know why you feel the way you feel, you should give yourself time to breathe and not get into any kind of communication with anyone. An anxious mind cannot think properly and it's going to reflect in your behavior. Instead of reacting to something in a weird way, it's better to relax and do something to cheer yourself up. You can try switching on your senses, such as smelling a nice fragrance, seeing something beautiful, listening to music, relishing a delicious meal, or squeezing a stress ball to calm your tensed muscles. You may try different ways to release stress and stick to whatever works for you.

Evaluating Somebody's Body Language

Understanding nonverbal cues can be very helpful in recognizing narcissists and knowing their selfish schemes. You may want to keep in mind the following points to make sure you don't get into any kind of relationship with people who might display narcissistic traits through their body language.

- A person's words and body language should match and not be opposite or inconsistent, meaning a person shouldn't say one thing and depict something completely different with their gestures, voice tone, and body movements. For example, if somebody says they really appreciate you, they shouldn't be looking away or checking their phone most of the time while talking to you.

- Don't just judge one particular body language of a person, but try to observe all their nonverbal signals collectively to understand their intent and attitude.
- As they say, eyes don't lie. Make sure you analyze the kind of eye contact the other person maintains. Is it a bit too much or just right?
- Notice the facial expressions. Is the face expressionless or is it full of interest?
- You should also try to sense who the person is by their voice. Is it warm, amicable, and confident or is there too much effort in the way they speak?
- Pay attention to how close they stand to you, as it shouldn't make you want to run away! Remember, people who are genuinely friendly and have good intentions never make you uncomfortable. They're respectful in the way they touch you and their gestures are absolutely nonintimidating.
- Above everything else, you should tune in to your gut feeling about a person. If you feel something isn't right, perhaps it's true. So, never ignore your instincts, as they can save you from a lot of potential trouble.

Remember, there's a difference between confidence and narcissism. There are people who know what they're capable of and they don't need anyone else's approval to feel confident about who they are. When you meet such people, they give you a very positive vibe and make you feel valued. On the contrary, people who are narcissists have fake confidence. They want everybody to praise them all the time so that they can stroke their pride and revel in their own fictional world of self-glory. When you meet such people, they give off a very negative vibe and make you feel as if your presence doesn't matter at all.

- A narcissist is always quick to criticize people, especially those who are of low status. If they're at a restaurant, they will be rude to waiters and attendants.
- Such people raise their voice and interrupt others to show they know better and others need to hear them out.

- Their body language changes—they begin to look down on whoever is there and attack with sharp movements and menacing gestures like hands in the air or above the waist.
- They also enjoy if somebody else is being demeaned or criticized. You'll often see a smirk and a wry smile on their face in such scenarios.
- When you're being attacked by a narcissist, you'll feel it quite clearly in your nervous system. You'll freeze and feel at a loss of words and if the other person is still not empathetic toward you, it's abuse.

Connection Between Your Mind, Emotions, and Body

So, to deal with a narcissist, you must work on your body language, as it can impact you on an emotional, physical, and mental level. Since your body and mind are interdependent, one will affect the other. For instance, if you are feeling anxious, your body will feel the anxiety, too. On the other hand, if you're happy and satisfied from within, your body will have a relaxed and confident stance. It's quite natural and you must use it to your advantage. Well, how do you do that?

Just like your body reacts to what your mind thinks, your mind also changes its thoughts according to your body language. For instance, if you're in a foul mood and someone drags you to dance to a piece of your favorite music, you'll begin to feel better in a while. According to some research, your facial expressions can also change your mood. If people had fewer frown lines and more smiles on their faces, they're likely to feel less anxiety.

Also, the way you walk can make a difference in your thoughts. If you walk reluctantly with hanging shoulders, it's going to make you think about all the negative stuff, while if you walk happily with an upright posture, it's going to make your mind think about all the positive things. When your body language is happy and confident, it helps you notice all the constructive things and appreciate the good in others. You'll not think about what you're not capable of, but you'll think about how you can improve what you're already good at.

Our bodies, minds, and emotions are all tied together. If one gets affected in any way, the other also reacts. Thus, we can make it work for our own good. If you feel a certain way, try readjusting your gestures, postures, and facial expressions. You have the power to improve your self-confidence and raise your happiness level by breathing more deeply, dancing, walking, laughing (watching something funny), and smiling.

Watch out for These Signs to Stay Away From Narcissists

Besides reading the body language of a person you meet for the first time, you should also watch out for certain warning signs, which can help you avoid dating or befriending a narcissist:

- A narcissist will only talk about themselves—their job, their vacation, their house, and their favorite pursuits. The moment somebody else tries to participate in the conversation, they seem to lose interest. They will stop making eye contact, start looking away, or check their phone. They'll give you a feeling that they don't care what you do and who you are.
- They naturally dominate and control even when they meet somebody for the very first time. For instance, if you meet them at a coffee shop, they may place your order without even consulting you or simply presume that you'll be okay with whatever they want to drink or eat.
- You'll hear them complain and grumble all the time about all sorts of petty things like long queues, food arriving late, or somebody's baby crying. This shows their inability to see the whole situation from a broad perspective and that they focus only on how it's causing inconvenience to them.

- They might just devalue your choice by criticizing it. For instance, if you've ordered a pizza, they may grab a bite and say that they've had better pizzas.
- Most narcissists are likely to have short-lived relationships due to their toxic behavior patterns. So, try to coax out insights about their past relationships.
- They like to fish for compliments. If they don't get them, they say things like "Oh, my outfit doesn't suit the occasion" or "I wish I had worn a different watch to go with my shoes." They say such inconsequential things to persuade the other person into praising them.
- They'll try to impress you by going the extra mile for you— present you an expensive gift, escort you to the bathroom, or drop you home. It's their tactic to cover up for their insecurity and try to appear nice.

Remember, if somebody is really confident, caring, and trustworthy, they don't need to show it. In fact, such people are humble and allow other people to share their opinions and perspectives.

So, now you know how to read people's body language, stay away from narcissistic personalities, and evolve into a more confident individual. The more you know about a narcissist and how they attract you initially, the better guarded you can be and avoid getting into a relationship with them.

Chapter 5:
Covertly Abused

There are lots of us who are abused in oblivion. We know something doesn't feel right, but we aren't able to identify it. To put it straight—anyone who attacks your self-esteem in any manner is your abuser. Abuse doesn't have to be covert all the time. It can be covert, too. When someone is covertly abused by somebody, they're being psychologically or emotionally shattered. The sad part is that covert abuse isn't as recognized as physical abuse because the former is not as visible as the latter. Unfortunately, a covert form of abuse is often consciously or unconsciously accepted by society, even though it's as dangerous as physical (or sexual) abuse. Thus, a person who suffers from it feels extremely lonely, which makes the situation even worse for them. In such relationships, the abuser invalidates key components (needs, desires, values, beliefs, opinions, and feelings) of an individual's personality and existence.

So, who exactly is the covert abuser? Well, they can be anybody—your spouse, partner, parent, child, sibling, friend, or any close family member. The covert abuser often likes to shame, criticize, and belittle their victim. They do it in a manner that the victim begins to feel confused about their own reality and beliefs. Since narcissists use mind games very skillfully, they're able to convince you that you're at fault even when you're not. Also, there are abusers who can be kind and nice to you on certain occasions and then again go back to being mean for no reason. So, it's a tricky kind of abuse.

It's hard for a person to even accept that they're being covertly abused because, in most scenarios, they're being abused by someone they're emotionally bound to. Nobody wants to have a bad opinion of someone they love. Therefore, most of the time, the victim chooses to remain silent. They feel scared to confront their abuser because they don't want to get into heated arguments, which could possibly lead to more pain and abuse. It's like being abused becomes a habit with time. The victim doesn't even realize that they have lost their own sense of individuality and personal power for the sake of accommodating their abuser. It's a state of codependency, which people find almost impossible to break free from. It can also be called relationship addiction. Even though the victim knows they're stuck in a miserable relationship, they can't seem to find a way out.

Codependency and Its Negative Effects

People who're part of dysfunctional families often have to succumb to codependency. The abuser likes to have their way all the time (or most of the time) while the codependent person submits to them without choice. They have no voice of their own and never express how they feel. There's no love, affection, care, or support in the relationship. On the other hand, there are frequent episodes of bullying, lying, blaming, lashing out, and calling names. When a codependent person lives in such an unhealthy and destructive atmosphere for years and years, they become sour from inside. They lose trust in people and even in themselves.

It's an extremely damaging situation because a codependent person gets used to taking responsibility for somebody else's actions. They tend to do more than they're supposed to and when their efforts aren't recognized, they feel hurt. They depend on relationships for their survival and live in constant fear of abandonment. They look for approval for anything and everything because there's no self-assurance to depend on. The worst part is that they have lots of bottled-up emotions, especially anger, which makes them mentally unstable. They sacrifice their own well-being for the sake of meeting the needs of another person.

A codependent person is barely themselves. They have poor self-esteem and have no connection to their inner self, which is why they're always looking for external ways to soothe their pain and find comfort. They may get into alcohol, drugs, gambling, or workaholism in an attempt to break away from it all, but seem to find no escape from the vicious cycle.

While emotional abuse can be found in all kinds of relationships, it's quite common in heterosexual married couples. The root of which stems from the patriarchal way of thinking that most men are conditioned with. They consider themselves to be superior to women in all respects, which is why they feel entitled to demand anything from their female counterparts without feeling obligated to reciprocate. Men who want to stay in control like to undermine, objectify, overburden, deprive, and degrade women. Even though women may have expertise, education, and personal attributes, they may still be mistreated just because they are women. In order to have dignity and respect for both genders in a relationship, it's important for them to understand that there's no need to devalue the other person.

To deal with covert manipulation and codependency, a person needs to come face to face with what's happening with them. The problem with emotional abuse is that everybody denies and suppresses it as long as possible. It's like the big elephant in the room that everybody chooses to turn a blind eye to. However, the sooner you address a problem, the easier it gets to deal with it. Most people don't realize that the more you delay confronting a wrong, the more chronic it gets and harder to eradicate.

There can be quite a few reasons for victims of any form of abuse to refuse (or pretend to be unaware of the abuse) to accept or realize the fact that they're being abused:

- Perhaps they come from an abusive background and they've gotten so used to it that they don't even consider abuse abnormal. They self-blame whenever their abuser finds fault with them and they simply try to work harder at being better.
- Most victims stay in abuse for so many years and adjust to it slowly without knowing they're being abused.
- They're just too ashamed to admit that they're being abused. They feel guilty about not being able to face it or for simply giving in to it foolishly.

Signs That Indicate Covert Abuse

Let's get down to understanding the signs and symptoms of covert abuse, so that we know when to be alarmed and protect ourselves.

Shaming and Mocking

The most common way of attacking somebody psychologically is by belittling them, which comes naturally to a covert abuser. They know what upsets you or makes you feel vulnerable and they hit you right there. They say things to mock and shame you, which may leave you feeling insulted and baffled. For instance, if you two are sitting in a family gathering, they may say, "You can't even toast a bread properly, there's no way you can prepare something as sumptuous as chicken steaks." Their idea is to show you in poor light to others.

Controlling Behavior

The abuser tries to control you so that they can have their way. In any given scenario, they like to overpower you by either playing the victim card or controlling your actions and decisions. For instance, they may want to complete your sentences and speak on your behalf when you're spending time with other people. Not just that, they may also restrict you or totally stop you from meeting your friends and family. They may tell you how to dress and comb your hair and even keep a check on how much you spend.

Slandering

Since covert abusers usually are quite likable, it's easy for them to turn other people against the sufferer. If the victim tries to walk out of a codependent relationship, their narcissistic abuser is most likely to defame them publicly. They may talk badly about the victim to their friends and family so that they may not believe the victim's side of the story.

A narcissistic person can totally deflect your charges of abuse, make you self-doubt, and feel lonely and helpless.

The Blame Game

A narcissistic person always finds something or the other wrong with everybody. In their opinion, everybody else is always unfair to them and they are being treated badly. It's their tactic to draw other people's attention and gain sympathy. They like to punish people who're emotionally attached to them by giving them the silent treatment. They often act hurt to indicate that the victim is at fault and that they're hard to please. Blaming others for everything that goes wrong is one of their strategies to conceal their weaknesses.

Shifting Responsibility of Their Bad Behavior onto the Victim

Covert abusers never take responsibility for their actions. When they get angry, abuse, yell, and demean the other person, they justify their abusive behavior by putting it on the person who's on the receiving end. They believe they have the right to misbehave because the other person enraged them. They simply disregard the abuse and put the victim in the spotlight.

Deviating From the Main Topic of Conversation

It's always frustrating to have a conversation with a narcissist who's a covert abuser, as they never get your point. They twist your words and misrepresent your feelings to make sure that they aren't proved wrong in an argument. They may say things like, "you can't be perfect," "am I so bad," or "as if you never make mistakes." You may feel exhausted after a while and may want to refrain from arguing any further.

Gaslighting

Gaslighting is the attempt to make someone doubt their own perception, memory, and reality. A narcissist typically tries to make their victim believe something that's false or something that never happened. They may also twist your words, misinterpret what you said, or completely deny what they said a few days ago. The victim begins to doubt their own understanding and eventually gives in to their abuser's manipulation.

Let's understand gaslighting (also called 'fact changing') with a story: A 27-year-old guy lived with a narcissistic father, who asked them to visit the bank and withdraw $150 for groceries. The son did exactly what they were asked to—they went to the bank, withdrew $150, and handed it over to their dad. Now, the following day, they went to the store, and it was all good until then. Three days later, the narcissistic father woke up the son to scream and accuse them of stealing money out of the bank account and causing overdraft fees. This led to a very long and drawn out argument. The fact of the matter was that the father had written a check to a person they owed money to and was embarrassed to admit so (and they really never did). The father denied going to the store with the son and even asked them to withdraw money. In fact, the father continued to bring up the matter again and again, and they changed the story each time to confuse their son and create self-doubt in their mind.

Making Negative Comments

Covert abusers say things to discourage other people and make them feel unloved, but they do it without taking the onus for their statement. For instance, they may say, "I like your dress, even though you look fat in it." They never praise or support anybody wholeheartedly. Making negative comments is their way of feeling stronger and more confident in themselves. The idea behind making the other person feel small is to aggravate them and prove that they can't even handle a joke.

Pretending to Be Forgetful

When somebody tries to convict covert abusers of their behavior, they pretend to have forgotten the incident or claim they never intended to do anything wrong. They act as if nothing happened, making the other person feel as if they're concocting a story. That's when the victim begins to feel clueless and helpless, not knowing what to do.

For instance, if you try to confront them for not helping you with a task even when they weren't busy, they may say something like, "Oh really! When did you ask me for help? I can't recall."

Denying Their Own Statements

Covert abusers deny saying things in the past or they twist their own words to suit what they want to imply in the current moment. If you try to reason with them, they simply claim that you don't remember things properly or misunderstood what was said. So, it's always complicated to discuss or resolve any issue with them.

It's a little different from gaslighting (which we've discussed earlier). For instance, they may have told you they never relished a particular kind of cuisine. However, on another occasion, they might simply complain about not getting to eat that very same cuisine that they once never relished. So, when you try to remind them of their original statement, it's likely to turn into an argument, which may leave you exasperated for no fault of yours.

Covert Emotional Abuse Caused to Children

Covert emotional abuse just doesn't happen to adults, it can happen to children as well. So, if you're with a narcissistic partner, make sure your children are safe. When we talk about child abuse, it's usually about physical or sexual abuse. However, emotional or psychological abuse is also equally damaging as it can impact your child's adult life.

Below are some of the kinds of emotional abuse a child can face:

- A child can feel emotionally neglected by their parents. When a child is growing up, their mind is like a blank canvas that can be painted with anything. Thus, it's important to build their confidence by showing them love and affection in a balanced way. Since children are full of curiosity, they ask a lot of questions and they also have their own perspectives on different things. It's imperative to answer their questions with intent and keenness and be respectful toward their opinions. If a parent rubs their child off the wrong way and ignores their feelings, it's emotional neglect.
- Some children are degraded and verbally abused by their elders, which haunts them all their lives. They begin to believe what they constantly hear about them. If they're told they are lazy, stupid, and incompetent, they will begin to feel that way. The kind of words and remarks children hear shape their thinking and help in brain development. When they receive negative comments or opinions, they aren't able to develop confidence. If they fail at even small things, it discourages them deeply.
- There's something called covert incest or enmeshment, which means an unhealthy closeness between a parent and their child. When a parent depends on their child for emotional support, which can be given by only a romantic partner, it's a form of emotional abuse. Such an association may or may not be sexual in nature, but a child may get

exposed to sexual matters quite early on, which isn't good for them and it may also impact their adult sexual life.

- Then there are children who're groomed for sexual exploitation. Sadly, such abuse is mostly caused by someone known to the child. The predator identifies their victims, wins their trust, and isolates them to be able to use them for their sexual gratification. The child doesn't even understand what they get into and it's hard for them to escape because they're so full of shame and fear.
- Humiliating and shaming children in front of others is also a kind of psychological abuse that is caused by many parents. It has such a deep impact on a child's emotional health that it continues to bother them even when they become an adult. They just aren't able to feel good about themselves. Some parents also play pranks on their children and expect them to take it in the right spirit, but they don't realize that children are innocent and they need constant reassurance and encouragement for their growth.

If children are hurt emotionally, the scars usually remain for a lifetime. Thus, each parent should be careful about how they treat their children. However, if you've had emotional damages in the past that seem hard to heal, there's definitely light at the end of the tunnel. While it may not be the easiest thing to cope with abuse, you can come out of it completely if you're determined and focused on it.

Healing Techniques

Recovery has to start with identifying a toxic relationship and choosing to end it. If you've been abused by somebody, it doesn't mean you have to stay that way all your life. Remember, it's normal to feel the pain and confusion while you decide to part ways with someone you love deeply. But you need to take the bold step of leaving your abuser and allowing yourself to move on. You can begin your life all over again with new hope and new expectations.

You need to ask yourself, "am I willing to set myself free?" If your answer is yes, there's nothing that can stop you.

Follow the strategies below to heal from narcissistic abuse:

Learn to Trust Yourself

Never doubt yourself when it comes to knowing why you're doing what you're doing. The saddest part about covert abuse is that it's not easily comprehended by most people. You may find yourself alone on the journey of your recovery. Therefore, you should trust your thoughts, feelings, and emotions. You need to empower yourself by constantly reminding yourself that you deserve to be happy.

Also, you might have to stand your ground even when everybody is seemingly against you and your abuser continues to accuse you falsely.

Label Your Emotions

It's important to dig deep into your inner world to be able to heal emotionally. Pay close attention to your gut feelings and instincts. Sit down quietly and identify the emotions you've inside of you—it could be anger, confusion, shame, guilt, and betrayal. Anyone who's manipulated feels invalidated. So, as soon as you come to terms with your emotions, break away from everything and stop interacting with your abuser.

Rejuvenate Yourself

After you've accepted your true emotions and feelings, it's time to rejuvenate yourself. You may indulge in activities like journaling, praying, meditating, or maybe talking to a friend. The idea is to get clarity of mind and be grounded in what you believe in.

Even if you don't want to end a narcissistic relationship, take a break from it to refresh your mind.

Practice Mindfulness

You can also practice mindfulness to train your mind to accept your experiences no matter how painful they've been, which is going to comfort you mentally and boost your happiness. All you have to do is sit quietly and bring your focus to the present moment and accept it without judgment. The more regularly you do it, the more effective it's going to prove. If you don't wish to do it on your own, you can reach out to a meditation expert to help you get started with it.

End All Contact With Your Abuser and Set Boundaries

Whether it's your ex-partner, parent, sibling, or a friend, decide to end your relationship with them in a way that you never see them again. Yes, you may feel tempted to speak to them once in a while or at least reply to their messages, but it's not going to help. You might even have to block them on social media, emails, and stop taking their calls. Remember, even one message or email can lead to a chain of more complexities and never-ending trouble. You need to set your personal boundaries and not let your abuser cross them.

Be Prepared for Post-Traumatic Stress Disorder (PTSD)

The transition from being in an abusive relationship to getting out of it isn't easy. In fact, it can be quite traumatic for the simple reason that it causes a lot of emotional pain. It's perfectly normal to go through emotions like anger, shock, and sadness. You may also feel fearful and anxious. So, it's better to be prepared for the trauma and seek professional support instead of dealing with it in a confused manner.

Remember, you may feel down and out for a period of time, but you will certainly come out of it completely. The brave decision to leave a narcissistic abuser can't be wrong, which should give you strength to sail through.

Rebuild Your Identity

When you've spent many years with a covert abuser, it can make you forget your true self. You may have stopped doing things that you liked because of your narcissistic partner's mean comments and controlling behavior. Thus, you need to explore your inner self all over again and form a new relationship with your own self. It's like you need to pick up fragments of your own being and become a whole person who's unique, special, and confident.

You may not want to get into a new relationship while you're still recovering from your past hurts and trying to reclaim your identity, as it may not prove to be healthy. You're likely to get hurt again or you may hurt the other person because you haven't dealt with your own pain yet.

Accept Your Feelings

You may continue to love the person who abused you and may like to fall back on the good memories created with them. It's okay to feel that way because you can't really force your emotions to change suddenly just because you've broken up with someone. Only time can heal the deep emotional wounds embedded within you. So, allow yourself to heal while you still have feelings for your ex-partner. You don't have to erase their existence from your mind to be able to move on. Knowing and accepting this can help you make better progress.

Stop Judging Yourself

You will feel sorry for yourself and may even blame yourself for your abuser's behavior. However, you need to remind yourself that there's no excuse for bad behavior and any kind of abuse. If a person is abusive, they need to take responsibility for their actions. You don't have to feel guilty or think that you could have done things differently. On the other hand, you should feel proud of yourself for ending an unhealthy relationship.

Practice Positive Affirmations

Saying positive things about yourself is powerful. Whenever you feel low and helpless, make affirmations like "I can do it," "I'm strong," and "I'm enough." By doing so regularly, you'll gain confidence and feel happier. You can also make it a routine to say at least a few positive words and phrases every day in the morning and just before you go to bed. The more positivity you'll ingrain in your mind, the sooner you'll be able to heal and find your new self.

Be in Good Company

Choose to spend time with supportive people. They could be your friends or family. Talking your heart out to people who're mature and sensitive can strengthen you emotionally and help you cope with your pain in a much easier way. However, be careful about people who might cause more hurt than comfort by blaming you for your abuser's behavior or simply invalidating your pain. Stay away from such folks!

Practice Self-Care

Since emotional trauma can take a toll on your physical and mental health, you should take care of yourself by eating balanced meals, sleeping for eight hours, going for walks, and pampering yourself with therapeutic treatments. You should also pursue your long-lost hobbies and connect with old friends. Self-care can improve your happiness level and increase the sense of self-worth within you.

Talk to a Therapist

You may want to speak to a professional who's trained to help you cope with your situation. Therapy can help you deal with anxiety, depression, and regulate your emotions. It can also help you come to terms with some of the hidden factors that make you more prone to abuse. Not just that, but you'll also be able to learn techniques to overcome thoughts of self-harm or reconnecting with your abuser.

Join a Community

Besides staying in touch with loved ones, you can also be part of a community of like-minded people. It can be a local church, fitness club, artists' association, or a volunteer group. If you can't seem to find an offline local community, you can join an online community, too. The purpose is to connect with people who have similar beliefs, passions, and goals in life. Think of your interests and the things that matter to you and reach out to a community accordingly. For instance, if you enjoy traveling, consider joining a travelers club or a camping group. Being a part of a community can aid in coping with stress and finding meaning in life.

Try Connecting With Somebody Who's Suffered Similar Abuse

Exchanging thoughts with somebody who's been or is in the same boat as yours is always comforting and can be enlightening, too. The kind of abuse the two people suffer may differ, but the pain and trauma are usually the same. Instead of talking to somebody who has no idea what you're going through or what you've been through, it's much more sensible to connect with somebody who knows exactly how you feel.

Perhaps both of you can come up with a solution to each other's problems or at least give each other the strength, the right insight into the matter, and the much needed hope.

Consider Traveling

Travel can contribute toward your healing as long as it's meaningful and introspective. It can help you shed your preconceived notions about the world at large. Thus, you can open up and mingle with different kinds of people, get acquainted with their belief system and priorities in life, which can help you put a lot of things in perspective. Going out and breathing in a totally new environment can be quite invigorating and therapeutic. Also, travel can help you regain your lost confidence because you get to make so many decisions on your own (choosing where to go, where to stay, and what to explore). You'll also get to form a lot of opinions of your own, which are going to be devoid of anyone's influence. So, it's a great way to rediscover yourself and reestablish your strength as an individual.

A Narcissist's Reaction to Losing Control Over Their Victim

Keep in mind, your abuser won't like losing control over you. Narcissists find it very hard to deal with the fact that you're on your path to recovery and freedom. They're never going to let you go so easily because you're the one who has been providing fodder for their low self-esteem, weak ego, and insecurities. Thus, you need to know how they might react to you making an exit from their life.

- They might suddenly pretend to change and do things to please you—buy you gifts or try to spend more time with you.
- They may apologize insincerely just for the sake of being with you again. However, they are actually sorry for the consequences of your decision to leave them—the feeling of abandonment and losing control.
- They might even say things like there's nobody who can love you more than they do and that you're making a mistake.
- Don't be surprised if they meet your friends, siblings, or whoever you're close to and try to win you back through them. They'll talk all good stuff about their relationship with you to convince them that there's no real problem between you two and that you're simply overreacting.
- They may also spread rumors about you to protect their own image. The moment they get this inkling that people will find out about their true character, they label you as manipulative, abusive, and selfish. They will reach out to possibly everybody you know, such as your friends on social

media, relatives, parents, coworkers, and bosses, to defame you.

- They may also use some of your acquaintances to snoop into your life, to know what you're up to.
- They may also accuse you of being narcissistic, manipulative, and gaslighting. For instance, if you're divorcing a narcissist and you need to discuss certain terms with them about the kids' custody, they might escalate the discussion to a fight and accuse you of yelling and demeaning them. It's their tactic to make you want to defend yourself and explain to them that you aren't really doing what they're accusing you of.

So, if you've been dealing with a narcissist and now have decided to give your life a fresh start, be sure to keep your emotional reactions in check because that's going to give them the upper hand on you. Remember to be firm with your decision and do whatever is best for you.

Healing is possible, and it's certain as long as you make wise choices and refuse to stay enslaved to abuse. The only big step you need to take is to end a harmful relationship. You cannot help yourself while you're still with your abuser. If somebody chooses to mistreat you, it's their choice and they need to bear the brunt for the same and not you. The earlier you recognize and acknowledge the signs of covert abuse that you've been undergoing, the sooner you can escape it. The journey of recovery is tough, but it's definitely worthwhile and rewarding in the end.

Chapter 6:
Ethical Dilemma

I s manipulation always bad? To answer that, we need to first understand the true meaning of the word. In simple words, manipulation is a tactic used to influence somebody to take a certain action. People also manipulate situations to achieve a certain goal. The meaning or purpose of manipulation has been twisted over the ages because most of the time, people manipulate others for their own benefit. Typically, when people are manipulated, they're being dragged into something that's not their agenda. Also, manipulation may not be very obvious all the time. Many times, people don't even realize they have been manipulated. However, manipulation isn't always harmful or unethical. It can be good for the person who is being manipulated. Yes, it may sound strange, but it's true.

The difference between negative and positive manipulation is that the former is coercion while the latter is persuasion. When you compel somebody to do something they don't want, it's unethical manipulation. For instance, if your spouse tells you to take up a job close to their office so that the two of you may get more opportunities to spend time together; however, their real intent is to keep an eye on you; it's not good for you or your relationship. In this scenario, your spouse isn't really seeking your good, but is trying to find ways to control you because of their hidden insecurity. On the other hand, when you persuade somebody to do something that they do want, it's ethical manipulation. For instance, if you plan a blind date for a friend of yours who you know is going to like the person you've chosen for them, it goes to show your genuine care and concern for them. You might not want to tell your friend that you're trying to infuse romance in their life, but you secretly want them to date a nice person.

Evaluate the Reason Behind Your Manipulation

Your intent and purpose are key to identifying the kind of manipulation you want to get into. If you aren't being selfish and not seeking your own good at the cost of harming or harassing the other person, you're on the right track. When you want to achieve something of value for the other person, it's a good manipulation. In fact, manipulation is part of everyone's life. Brands and companies manipulate consumers to buy their products. They don't tell you plainly to choose their goods and services over others. Instead, they use the technique of manipulation to make you believe that if you go with what they produce, your life will get better. Now, such manipulation can be good or bad for you. That's something that you, as a buyer, have to decide. There are brands that promote a healthy lifestyle and they sell products that are overpriced and often not as healthy as they claim to be, so if you still decide to incorporate them in your lifestyle, it may do you more harm than good.

Social Manipulation

There's something called social manipulation that not many of us are familiar with, but it's fascinating. It actually means to be resourceful, creative, and helpful. If you're someone who manages to adjust to what's happening around you, so that it results in something meaningful, you know how to manipulate well. In fact, being manipulative is the foundation of every discovery and innovation that the human mind could think of. It's the cause of the motivation that led us to the modern age. Everything evolved and progressed due to manipulation. If the human mind wouldn't have thought of manipulating wood to turn into building materials, we wouldn't be where we are today. The human mind manipulated grains to make bread, fire to prepare meals, and so on. So, manipulation is a life skill that we've had ingrained in us right from the beginning. It's not something we need to acquire. It's there within us. We need to activate it for the betterment of everyone. If you use manipulation in a positive way, you can make life more fulfilling for you and everyone around. You need to do something good and influence others to follow in your footsteps.

Remember, everybody likes to be with people who they can relate to. Nobody wants to be around those who appear to be perfect or almost angelic. We all have flaws and it's alright. All you need to do to make a positive impact in the world is to be a genuine and humble person—try to engage with people sincerely and not just pretend to listen when they talk to you. Don't just blabber about yourself, but be curious to know other people and their good traits. It's a great way to live a life of meaning and purpose.

You have the power to create a good or a bad day. So, try to be someone that builds people up (encourages and motivates them to pursue their goals). Don't criticize or demean people. It leads to nothing valuable. Instead, highlight the victories and plus points of a friend. However, don't be generic with your praise. Try to be specific and honest, so that your compliment helps everyone.

When you're talking to your peers or anybody for that matter, make sure to acknowledge their opinions. Try to listen with focused attention. Don't be afraid to talk about your flaws because this can warm the coldest of hearts and help you win unexpected support.

Most of us don't know how to empathize without offering instructions. We simply don't get it that when somebody needs to be emphasized with, they don't need advice. They just need empathy. So maybe you want to practice empathizing by not concocting solutions when someone simply wants to vent out their honest thoughts. Remember, the person who's in distress is also capable of solving their problem, but they need to be heard. You need to acknowledge what they're undergoing is really bad before you rush into rescuing them.

Keep in mind that each person is complex, vulnerable, and unique. You may see them as tough, educated, and outgoing individuals, but they all need support and listening ears once in a while. You can use manipulation to uplift people and foster your life purpose.

Manipulation Can Bring Positive Change

Positive manipulation is a great tool used by non-profit organizations and all kinds of ethical brands to induce people to make noble choices, help the needy, and promote goodness in the world. For example, there are many social organizations and NGOs that use persuasion to inspire people to donate stuff, become fundraisers, and propagate ideas that can make people aware of issues that need immediate attention and action.

While an average manager likes to control their team by threatening them, a good manager tries to keep their team members engaged and inspired. It's a significant aspect of professional growth for employees, which comes with several benefits for both the individual and the organization on the whole.

So, manipulating your staff to perform excellently is an ultra efficient management tool, which can result in employees achieving their goals and enabling teams to accomplish organizational milestones.

Behavioral Change

Then there are manipulations like influencing somebody to quit smoking, go on a diet for weight loss, or take therapy for mental wellness. So, whatever you want to help somebody with has to benefit the other person without any of your own selfish personal gain. For instance, if you take a family member on a vacation with a clandestine agenda of making them join a therapy center that helps people quit all kinds of addictions, it's clearly for their good. It may not sound right to not to tell somebody your true intent behind an action and get them in a situation they weren't aware of or prepared for, but if it proves to be helpful in bringing them freedom from an addiction, they may thank you eventually for what you did for them. So, the outcome of anything you strategize for others' matters.

Unconventional Strategic Influence

Does manipulation always have to be transparent and honest? As stated earlier, you can take a loved one on a trip with a hidden agenda of persuading them to take therapy for quitting an addiction. If you tell them in a straightforward manner that they need to do something to quit a harmful habit, they may not listen to you and continue to be addicted. Remember, your objective is not to make them succumb to your will, but to break their adamant and irrational defenses.

Here's a hypothetical situation to understand how ethical manipulation can turn opposition into cooperation:

For instance, person A is aware of person B's turmoil in dealing with a bad relationship due to which they aren't able to cope with the challenges of their professional life and they also have poor finances. Person B clearly needs help in terms of understanding their mental situation and ways to overcome it. Since person A is a good friend of person B, the former is trying hard to convince the latter to take professional counseling to be able to stabilize their mind and move on with life in a progressive manner. However, they've no clue about what they're undergoing and neither do they have any inclination to resolve it. Now person A has a scheme in place to persuade person B to take help, which they have been refusing—they concoct a story that relates to person B's situation—they tell them about one of their cousins who had a painful divorce at quite a young age and they also lost their job. After being miserable for a few years, the cousin finally agreed to get professional therapy, which helped them come out of their trauma way faster and think of new ways to rebuild their life. The counseling and therapy didn't just help them change their thought patterns from pessimistic to more optimistic, but also motivated them to meet new people, form new friendships, and enjoy life.

Person A, very skillfully, fabricated an anecdote to make person B believe that doing something fruitful was important to be able to defeat their negative state of mind. Of course, mental health experts can't change your circumstances, but they can certainly give you clarity on how you should think and act. So now person B understands the value of mental well-being and they have given in to the persuasion of person A.

In the above scenario, person A's decision to trick person B into doing something that they weren't ready for can be thought of as something downright deceptive and dishonest, but it's also a clever strategy to nudge someone toward their betterment. Thus, such scheming can't be termed as immoral. It's rather an act of compassion and care. Person A might have used devious tactics, but their underlying motives were undoubtedly upright and practical, too.

So, you can come up with a variety of instances, where you can have a more creative and tactful approach to instigate someone's welfare rather than going for a traditional approach, which might not be effective.

According to a book titled *Paradoxical Strategies in Psychotherapy: A Comprehensive Overview and Guidebook*, almost all eminent schools of therapy comprised various unconventional methodologies that might not come across as acceptable or conforming to the prevalent norms. Therefore, some therapists refrained from using those paradoxical ideas for the fear of being misunderstood as deceitful. However, there's an important point to comprehend before we write off such devices— they can cajole people to get on the path of mental recovery. So, it would be rather unethical to ignore such techniques, especially when there seems to be no way out for the person who's suffering and seemingly helpless.

Manipulation and Leadership

Manipulation helps you to be a good leader. It's a smart way of concealing information from your followers and dealing skillfully with their emotions, insecurities, and weaknesses. It's not bad to manipulate as long as it's for the betterment of the one being influenced. For example, if you lie to your spouse about a surprise vacation, it isn't bad, right? Perhaps it's good for renewing the declining intimacy.

So, whatever manipulative strategies you carve out, to whatever degree, it should produce something fruitful for the maximum number of individuals. An ethical decision is defined solely by its outcome, and not by what's supposed to be right.

We all are leaders in our own right. Be it at the workplace, in a group of friends, or in our households, we need to make decisions, resolve conflicts, and work toward people's well-being. Therefore, we all need to manipulate; what matters is the purpose of manipulation—we need to ask ourselves if we're manipulating for our own good or to benefit others. Without constructive manipulative tactics, it's impossible to succeed as leaders.

Manipulating a Narcissist

Although manipulation is a narcissist's tool to get what they want from everybody else, you can also use it to make peace with them. Yes, you can't really change the way narcissists behave with you, but you can certainly have a strategic approach to your communication with them. The purpose of manipulating a narcissist should be to keep them calm and avoid heated arguments as much as possible.

Remember, you don't have to manipulate a narcissist to get them out of your way or to get something from them. The goal is to keep the relationship mutually agreeable, peaceful, and possibly rewarding. If you manage to achieve that with a person who has narcissistic traits, it's beneficial for the both of you.

Below are some of the manipulative ways to handle a narcissist:

- Keep your expectations realistic with a narcissist. Don't expect them to understand your point of view in an argument.
- Avoid criticizing them. If you criticize a narcissist, you enrage them. Instead, compliment them for something they're good at. Make sure compliments sound genuine and not over-the-top. However, be careful how you compliment a vulnerable narcissist because their brain processes a conversation in a different way. They like to replay everything that people say to them, which may make them disregard your compliment as fake.
- Stop being stunned or disgusted at their behavior. Narcissists are the most predictable folks. So, you need to have a radical acceptance of who they are. The more aware you're of their reality, the better guarded you can be.
- Try to empathize with their lack of empathy. For example, to empathize with their dominant nature, you can say something like, "It's good that you take charge of things. If you don't act this way, things might not move."
- Never defend yourself if you happen to get accused of something. The more defensive you get with a narcissist, the deeper you get in the chaos of an argument with them, which is of no use. So, for instance, if they accuse you of getting late for an appointment while you were right on time, say something like, "Let's just start right now."
- Offer to help a narcissist with something they're trying to accomplish. For instance, if you see them working on a project, you may say something like, "I see that you've so many responsibilities to take care of. Can I help you with

this?" When you help them, they might want to help you with your tasks, too.

- Be aware of their triggers and try your level best to avoid saying anything that might offend them or make them feel insecure. Remember, narcissists have very low self-esteem. Thus, when they feel their weak area is being attacked, they react in anger.
- Take responsibility for your action and be quick to apologize. For instance, if a narcissistic friend or a family member complains, "You've been too busy to even congratulate me on my new car!" You can immediately own up to that and say, "I know I lost track of time last week and forgot to congratulate you. I'm sorry about that."
- Disengage with a narcissist instead of showing that you're affected by their annoying remarks or bullying. No matter how pathetic you feel, stay unresponsive and unaffected— that's how you outsmart them.

Be aware, though, the idea behind these strategies is not to make a narcissist a better narcissist. You don't have to take responsibility to supply to them what they seek the most—an ego boost—to feel superior to others. You need to be cautious about how you interact with them, because that's going to help you stay calm. Also, you must keep in mind that trying to make peace with a narcissist doesn't mean you're undermining your personal power. Whenever you have to deal with a narcissist at any point in time, you need to remind yourself that they need to be treated like a child. So, you should be ready to lose a few battles in order to win the war.

Chapter 7:
Can it Be Done? Changing a
Narcissist

I n a typical sense, getting rid of narcissism isn't a cakewalk. Whether you're coping with a narcissist or suffering narcissism yourself, it's difficult to eradicate it from your life. Perhaps you can heal your own narcissism, but unfortunately, you cannot change another narcissist. A narcissist can change only if they realize that they have a problem and that they need to do something about it. They need to be aware of their own narcissism and its negative effects. Also, they should earnestly desire to abandon it, which is quite improbable because narcissists typically don't believe they can ever be wrong. In a narcissist's mind, they're always right. However, there's still hope. To help a narcissist heal, you need to first know the root of their narcissism.

There are people who're generally self-obsessed, manipulative, and unabashedly entitled. You may not want to try to change them because that's how they are, and it's never sensible to expect someone to stop being who they truly are. Keep in mind that you simply have no control over how the other person behaves. No matter how closely related you are to a narcissistic person—they could be your spouse, sibling, parent, or child, you can't take responsibility for their thoughts and actions. If they choose to be a certain way, it's their prerogative and they need to bear the brunt for their own decisions. You should rather try to protect your own identity and self-esteem if you're with someone who simply doesn't care about your feelings and likes to hurt them quite often to boost their own ego. Sometimes people inherit certain character traits from their parents or they simply grow up in an environment that makes them absorb narcissism in such a natural way that they can't seem to even know that it's not normal or it's rather dangerous.

Since narcissists are of various kinds and narcissism can also result from abusive and traumatic early life of a person, you can choose to help them heal their wounds. Any person who has been through pain and hurt in their past tries to keep themselves guarded behind the facade of arrogance and aggression. So, if you feel you're with someone who had an unfair past and they have been demeaning you because of their own bottled up bitterness, you may want to aid them in escaping their deep insecurity and fear of never being good enough. That being said, you must disengage in situations that are damaging to you, meaning you should set boundaries and not let the other person attack you emotionally, verbally, or physically.

Remember, you're precious and you deserve to be safe, happy, and thriving, which is possible only in a positive environment. Therefore, you must be confident and should tell a narcissistic loved one that you love them for who they really are, but you're not going to take their nastiness. You must also accept that not all narcissists can heal or change, and that you might have to take a tough call and make an exit from a relationship if it's not helping you become the person that you're supposed to be. There's no harm in being optimistic and pressing on for healing for a loved one, but you need to understand that they need to take the onus for their treatment. If they have no willingness to change, you can't do anything about it and you shouldn't waste your time, energy, and efforts on such a person. The more you invest your emotions in someone who has no awareness or inclination toward their problem, the more frustrated you'll feel and stay far from your own life goals. Why would you want that?

Stop Being Manipulated

As someone who's living with a narcissistic person, you must ensure that you don't compromise on your own mental well-being and stifle your personal growth. Your priority shouldn't be to heal or change a narcissistic husband or wife, boyfriend or girlfriend, or anybody, for that matter. You shouldn't feel obligated to be with them even if they are being inconsiderate in their ways. You should stop feeling guilty for someone else's wrong behavior. If someone makes you feel you're inadequate or you make them mad doesn't mean it has to be so. You should be confident about who you are and stick to your own beliefs and value system irrespective of what your narcissistic significant other says. You can reassure them that you love them for who they are, but you don't have to agree with everything they have to say or do.

Some Narcissists Will Never Change and It's Okay

You should save yourself from being manipulated. You may not realize it, but manipulation is quite common in most relationships. Sometimes it's for your benefit, while sometimes it's not good for you. A person with NPD tries to manipulate you for their own advantage. They can go to any length to convince you that you're in the wrong and that it's you who needs to change. You may feel isolated, bullied, and worthless. To recognize when you're being manipulated, you may want to watch out for signs like dishonesty, verbal abuse, gaslighting, threatening, stopping you from meeting your own loved ones, or showing passive-aggressive behavior. If you find yourself being manipulated in a relationship, you should refuse to succumb to their demands and try to deviate the conversation to a different topic. You can handle manipulation politely by staying calm and confident. No matter how hard the manipulator tries to make you believe something false, you need to stick to what's true. You can also address the situation head on by telling them that their behavior is manipulative and that it's not going to work on you.

Some people who have mental health issues use manipulation as a weapon to feel secure in their relationships. Thus, a therapist may help them address the real issue and educate them that manipulation isn't healthy.

Heal Your Own Narcissism

While it's pretty normal to seek one's own good and be selfish, it can be termed as "narcissism" when selfishness is found in a heightened degree. All humans are typically born selfish. Children are mostly self-centered because they don't know the value of caring for others yet. As they grow up, they learn to understand the meaning of considering the needs of others. However, there are some people who continue to be self-obsessed all their lives. The older they grow, the more selfish they become, because it can be quite addictive. The more you care just for yourself and use others for your own benefit, the more pleasurable it gets. A narcissist feels great about focusing on their own needs and desires. They gain more confidence and feel more powerful when they ignore other people's needs and have their way. However, such an attitude is bad for nurturing relationships. A hardcore narcissist doesn't typically have too many friendships to speak of. Even if they have friends, they're also narcissists.

A narcissist will not have many people by their side, eventually. It's a hard truth that any person with narcissistic traits must understand and accept. They may flourish in their own heads and bask in their own glories, but will remain clueless about real happiness and contentment. Thus, it's important to heal your own narcissism. Remember, it's in your hand! The first step is to be aware of it and then take action toward treating it.

Below are some of the helpful ways to cure narcissism within you:

- Try steering your attention from your own thoughts, feelings, opinions, and desires to other people. If you find it really hard to engage in a conversation with somebody because you already know what to speak, how to respond, and are always ready to judge, analyze, and draw conclusions, take a moment to breathe and be intentional about listening to the other person.

- Begin to care for more people around you. Treat it like a project and think about what you truly care for. If it's just you and your needs, there's a problem and you must address it. You may want to train your mind to think about what your spouse, children, and friends need from you. Look for opportunities to show them love and compassion. The more purposeful you become about caring for others, the better you'll feel about yourself.

- We all have our trigger points—things that upset and annoy us quickly. However, it's never helpful to react to situations in a huff and escalate matters. If you're someone who feels insulted and angry easily, you need to work on your emotions. You may want to practice mindfulness in order to regulate your feelings better and restore calmness during anxious times.

- Expand your network and be genuinely interested in knowing people of all kinds. Ask questions to make people feel valued and important. For example, you may want to get into conversations that dive into people's life dreams, passions, and things they care about. Share a few things about yourself and don't be afraid to reveal your vulnerable side. Let people know the real "you." When you make efforts to build authentic connections, you'll be less self-obsessed and find more love.

While it's possible to get rid of your narcissistic attitude and embrace a more balanced approach toward self-love and loving others, it's not something you can achieve in a day. It takes a lot of patience and understanding to go through the healing process. So, you need to be prepared to stay persistent and not give up, no matter how you feel.

Helping a Narcissistic Person Heal

There are relationships that have the potential to improve over time as long as there's respect and willingness to change. Thus, it makes no sense to call somebody a jerk or criticize their behavior, as it only makes them worse. However, they have better chances of improving when they're tenderly reminded of the value of their relationships and the strength they provide for them to accomplish their goals. If you're married to a person who has NPD, you'll need to figure out the intensity of the disorder and to what level it's been affecting your life. If you're constantly being abused and demeaned to the extent that you've begun to develop a low self-image, it's time to leave. In such a scenario, rebuild who you are and find what you want in life. Everyone deserves that and don't let anyone take that away from you. On the other hand, if you're convinced that you want to stay in a relationship with a narcissist or help a narcissistic family member get treated, you should try to understand their emotional wounds.

Be Compassionate and Understanding Toward Their Pain

Most narcissists are emotionally broken people. If a person has been through a lot of emotional pain, especially as a child, they're going to be wary of anything that would make them feel hurt again. If someone has been abandoned by their own parents, they usually live with the fear of abandonment. So, they choose to be mean to everybody. Their bad behavior is their protective gear that they put on to feel safe and powerful.

You should talk about the importance of your relationship and unleash your own feelings. You can do that by saying things like, "You're really precious to me" or "I care about our relationship" or "I want the best for you." Such statements can make a great deal of difference in the way your partner responds to your love. Of course, you need to practice what you preach and be careful about not doing the opposite. The more you strengthen your reassuring words with actionable support, the better chances you have of melting your narcissistic partner's heart toward you.

Also, try to think about the relationship holistically and focus on nurturing each aspect of it—steer your priorities from 'you and me' to 'we.' Since narcissists have deep insecurities, secure love can be their greatest necessity. If a narcissistic person truly wants to change, empathy can help them get rid of their bad habits and spiteful ways. That said, you shouldn't wear yourself out trying to fix someone who has full-fledged NPD. It can have an adverse effect on your emotional and mental state. They're out of your hand for sure and need professional help to improve.

You must also realize that not all narcissists have the same background of hurt and pain. For instance, if one narcissist is highly sensitive to jokes about how they appear, the other narcissist might not care about it at all. So, you might have to observe them closely before you decide how you want to help them.

Also, you will need to convince them of certain things before you persuade them into treatment or therapy. For instance, you'll have to assure them that you've no intention of harming or hurting them. If your narcissistic spouse feels threatened whenever you spend more time with other men/women, you can reassure them that you're not going to leave them. However, it has to be displayed in action and not merely in words. For example, you can spend more quality time with them and make future plans that speak about the two of you accomplishing something meaningful together.

Help Them Overcome Disagreement to Therapy

The biggest challenge to overcome in regards to a narcissist's healing is their disagreement and lack of openness to therapy and treatment. Most narcissists refuse to get treated because of their oblivion to their mental issues. Then there are some who enter therapy but don't stick to it because it's hard for them to self-reflect and shed their defenses. They also tend to feel that it's a waste of time and attention to seek any kind of therapy. Besides, if they're pushed into an inappropriate therapy, it may cause them more harm than good. Thus, you need to be careful about the kind of therapy you choose for them.

An NPD therapy typically includes:

- helping a narcissistic person overcome objection to therapy,
- identifying detrimental behaviors and defense mechanisms,
- analyzing reasons for narcissistic behaviors,
- exploring the negative effects of narcissistic behavior on other people,
- giving up grandiose thought patterns and being deliberate about thinking more objectively,
- adapting to new behavioral patterns, and
- acknowledging the outcome of positive behaviors.

Types of NPD Therapy

As stated earlier, it's important to pick the right kind of therapy for someone who might possibly have NPD. Also, the concerned person must be willing to give their time, attention, and focus to the treatment for at least a few years. They may feel significantly better after a few months (or maybe a year) and may get tempted to quit. However, it's vital to continue to take sessions for years and years until you're confident of being completely out of narcissism or at least achieving a profound change.

You may want to consider the following therapies to help someone cure their NPD:

Cognitive Behavioral Therapy (CBT)

The idea of CBT is to replace negative thought patterns and attitudes with positive ones. It's a psychological tool used by a therapist to help the client practice constructive skills to be able to develop healthy behavioral patterns over a period of time. A client is also given assignments to practice newly learned skills.

There are several CBT techniques like role playing, journaling, cognitive restructuring and reframing, situation exposure, relaxation, activity scheduling, mindfulness, and guided discovery that help in regulating emotions, solving difficult issues, facing hardships, and achieving goals.

Psychotherapy

Psychotherapy is a kind of talk therapy that helps a person understand their own emotions and feelings in a deeper way and eventually know the reason behind their behavioral patterns. When you come to terms with your past and your thoughts and emotions in the present day, it helps you manage your feelings, which gives you clarity on how to react to them in the best possible way.

Gestalt Therapy

Gestalt therapy is meant to bring a person's mind to what's happening in their life in the present rather than what existed in their past or what could happen in the future. It's a self-awareness therapy that helps in taking charge of one's life. Since each individual is driven by their present environment, Gestalt therapy helps them trust and accept how they feel.

When a person has a clear understanding of their thoughts, feelings, and behavior, they're able to form new perspectives and make positive changes in their life.

Schema Therapy

The idea behind schema therapy is to integrate the elements of psychotherapy with CBT techniques. The client is persuaded into recognizing and understanding unhealthy patterns and coping mechanisms that developed from their early childhood incidents.

Once the client is able to unveil these maladaptive schemas, they're taught to change or eradicate them. Of course, a person can't achieve it in a day. It needs practice and focus. If the client is sincere and consistent with their therapy, they can discover positive ways to nourish their emotional needs and modify their behavior and attitude toward others.

Transference-Focused Psychotherapy (TFP)

The TFP requires the client to redirect their emotions about someone toward the therapist and bare their heart openly. It's a technique to help the client understand their own thoughts, emotions, and feelings in a clearer way. Most of the time, we misunderstand our own emotions and fail to manage them. With the help of TFP, a person can be in touch with their real selves and learn to self-reflect rather than to judge others.

Mentalization-Based Therapy (MBT)

MBT can help in improving a person's ability to look within and also understand the thoughts and feelings of others before reacting. It's a technique that tells you how to connect emotions to behavior patterns or how emotions affect how we act. There's always a particular intent behind a person's behavior. So, everybody has a choice to analyze emotions and behaviors more wisely and not impulsively.

Metacognitive Interpersonal Therapy (MIT)

MIT is a systematic way of treating and dismantling narcissistic behaviors by addressing problems as they relate to a person's life, identifying maladaptive patterns and interpersonal abilities, and instigating positive change by motivating them to move away from old behavior patterns and foster new adaptive patterns.

Additionally, the therapist finds any possible barriers to efficacious therapy and tries to remove them.

Dialectical Behavior Therapy (DBT)

DBT is a kind of CBT, which includes sessions on mindfulness, stress management, emotion regulation, and interpersonal skills. DBT can have individual and group therapy sessions to help clients learn and practice new coping techniques. It can be a really effective therapy for anyone looking to heal their own narcissism.

Eye Movement Desensitization and Reprocessing (EMDR) Therapy

EMDR therapy aims to reduce the impact of negative memories of all kinds that a person might have been living with for years. Since it's assumed that narcissism has its roots in the early life experiences or traumas of a person, EMDR therapy is a systematic approach to taking the client into eight different phases. As the therapy progresses, the client is taken into the zone where they're supposed to face the memories of their dreadful past and emotional pain points.

The therapist directs eye movements to deviate the client's attention as and when they slip into the "negative memory" zone.

The key to total freedom from narcissism lies in motivating someone to see how positive change can help them live a more rewarding and successful life. You can also encourage them to explore the possible reasons behind narcissistic defenses. However, you need to do it without being critical or judgmental. Also, don't forget to offer validation and encourage self-forgiveness, self-belief, and self-compassion to help them get over their shame and vulnerability.

Narcissistic behaviors are bad because they affect your relationships in a bad way, which impacts the quality of your overall life. Therefore, a suitable therapy should be your priority to be able to change these behaviors for your own good. If you think you may have narcissistic behaviors but aren't sure about it, you should consider meeting a mental health professional for personality assessment. It's better to start treatment as soon as you discover tendencies toward narcissistic behavior, so that it doesn't become chronic and you're not enslaved by it. Therapy can enlighten you about a lot of things, which most people aren't able to perceive due to their lack of awareness.

Lastly, you must keep three key strategies in mind to deal with narcissism (whether it's your own personality disorder or someone else's): awareness, acceptance, and treatment. If you've managed to recognize your own narcissistic behavior, you should educate yourself about it and try to be mindful of not falling into its trap. You should seek treatment as soon as possible. However, if you're in a relationship with a narcissist, you should not try to argue, fight, or try to change them. You need to educate yourself about how to live peacefully with a narcissist (if you don't have the option of leaving them). However, if the relationship is abusive and tormenting, you should seek help without delay. Remember, it's never too late to improve your life, make changes, and get a new direction.

Conclusion

I f you've read the book from cover to cover, you know that you can defeat narcissism! It's not something that has the power to engulf your personality and existence. You definitely have a choice to kick it out of your life. Whether you've narcissistic traits in you or you're closely related to a narcissist, you can break free from it. Remember, there is hope and help. You don't have to accept narcissism! Sure, your situation could be grim and there might not be a way out. Perhaps you've almost lost your mind. But if you apply the techniques shared in this book, sincerely and consistently, you'll win the battle, eventually. However, it has to start from where it all began, meaning you need to explore the roots of a person's narcissistic behavior. When you know what creates narcissism and why a narcissist behaves the way they do, you'll gain better clarity and direction on how to tackle it and save yourself from its negative influences. If you don't know why something exists and try to solve it, you'll simply be going round and round with the problem and reach nowhere.

So, dig deep into narcissism. Talk to experts, read books (like the one you've just read), and try to get hold of some of the studies done on narcissism and NPD. Besides learning about the background and history of a narcissist abuser, you also need to know the kind of narcissist they are. You must know about the two main types of narcissists—grandiose and vulnerable—both of them are quite dangerous to be with. They both lack empathy for other people and are self-centered. While the grandiose narcissist has a sense of superiority and they like to have lots of people around (just for the glorification of their achievements), the vulnerable narcissist has a sense of inferiority and they try to run away from people (they're just too scared to be exposed and humiliated). Both types of narcissists need validation from the world for who they are. It's just that one asks for it all the time while the other one seeks it secretly. The bottom line is that they both make life miserable for people around them because of their selfish motives and behavior patterns. All kinds of narcissists believe that the people around them—parents, children, brothers, sisters, friends, coworkers, or even strangers—are supposed to be at their service.

There are many manipulative tactics that narcissists use to control those who share a relationship (personal or professional) with them. Manipulation is something that comes naturally to them. They make you think and act a certain way, and if you don't, they show their rage and how! From criticizing, demeaning, and ridiculing you to stonewalling and gaslighting, they do everything to make you doubt your own identity and beliefs. It's simply impossible to argue with a narcissist because they believe they're always right about everything. They're excellent at twisting words, changing facts, and maneuvering the conversation in their favor. You shouldn't be surprised if you begin to question your own reality, and feel frustrated, helpless, and clueless.

Narcissists find their way into your heart by first wooing you with their flattery and promises. They are usually charmers, at least in the beginning of a relationship; however, as soon as you form a solid relationship with them, it's time for them to reveal their true character. They begin to play all kinds of mental games with you to gain power over you. While some relationships are psychologically or emotionally abusive, narcissists can abuse their partners physically, too. The worst part is that there are so many people who aren't even aware that they're being abused. This is because narcissism is hard to identify. People who're narcissists may appear absolutely normal and even kind, which creates more confusion and helplessness for the victim.

Therefore, it's important to recognize the signs and symptoms of narcissistic abuse in a relationship as early as possible. Also, you must know how to tackle the dark psychology manipulation instead of being the victim. As stated earlier, it's never wise to get entangled in an argument with a narcissist. You should rather focus on protecting your mental health by sticking to facts and your beliefs, no matter what they say. Remember, you have the power to subdue their false claims as long as you're confident of who you are. You don't have to stoop to their lies about how they make you feel about yourself. Their nastiness is the blueprint of their own shame and insecurity. So, you don't have to feel embittered by their words or actions.

Besides, it's always better not to get into any kind of relationship with a narcissist. You can save yourself from a narcissist by knowing their personality type and the kind of body language they have. So whenever you're at a party or any kind of scenario where you've a chance of meeting new people, you should be watching out for those nonverbal cues and staying away from anybody who might seem to be narcissistic. You don't just have to read their body language, but you also have to give them the right signals, so that they don't prey on you. Of course, if you have narcissistic parents or other significant family members, you can't break your relationship with them so easily. But you can certainly draw your boundaries and not allow them to harm you. That said, you can always choose to detach yourself from a relationship if it gets toxic.

If you're covertly abused, it's time you take those indications seriously and get out of such a relationship. You don't have to underestimate emotional abuse just because the scars it leaves aren't visible. It's as damaging as any other kind of abuse (physical or sexual). Thus, you should reach out for help and begin to work toward your recovery. No matter how long you've lived with your abuser, you'll be able to heal your wounds and become a whole new person! It's just that you need to make the choice of leaving your narcissistic partner, spouse, parent, or best friend.

Also, manipulation isn't wicked per se. It's the intent and outcome that defines the nature of manipulation. So, don't fall for a narcissist's manipulation because it's always meant for your harm. Instead, use it to help them get on the right path. You can manipulate a narcissist to get therapy and change their ways for their own good. But of course, it has to be their own willingness and desire. There's a difference between persuasion and coercion. You can't make somebody do what they aren't convinced about, so you shouldn't even try that.

If you'd like to treat your own narcissism, you can start the journey right away! It's the best decision of your life. However, you need to be patient with yourself as it's a really long and slow process and there will be lots of backsliding. So, you don't have to lose heart, but be persistent with your efforts until you experience complete healing. As far as helping someone else come out of narcissism is concerned, you've a limited role to play. It's their decision and they need to understand that there's a problem. Keep in mind, narcissists live in their own bubble where they believe they don't need any help.

You may want to live with a narcissist because the relationship isn't abusive or toxic. You love them and they love you, too. In such a scenario, you can motivate them for professional counseling and therapy. If they agree to get treated and make sincere efforts to change, you can probably live together. In most scenarios, however, a narcissist won't be able to change. So, you need to make a decision based on your unique situation. If you're suffering abuse of any kind, in any measure, and it's affecting you as an individual, you must cut all ties with the abuser. You don't have to ruin your own identity and self-esteem for the sake of helping somebody heal, especially if they're unwilling to change and are continuing to harm you.

If this book helped you gain some perspective on narcissism and if you've found the strength to fight against it to be able to become the person you'd like to be, please leave a review on Amazon so that others can benefit from it, too.

References

41 Manipulation Tactics Used By Narcissists, Psychopaths, And Sociopaths. (2021, March 20). Abuse Warrior. https://abusewarrior.com/toxic-relationships/narcissistic-abuse/manipulation-tactics/

Bennett, T. (2019, September 6). *How do narcissists control you? What techniques do they use?* - Thriveworks. Counseling and Life Coaching - Find a Counselor. https://thriveworks.com/blog/how-narcissists-control-you/

Brown, L. (2020, July 14). *The art of positive social manipulation.* Medium. https://loribrown702.medium.com/the-art-of-positive-social-manipulation-8a100a564f17

Chinn, K.-A. (2016, July 9). *Can manipulation be used in a positive way?* - Go1. www.go1.com. https://www.go1.com/blog/post-can-use-manipulation-good

Codependency. (n.d.). Mental Health America. https://www.mhanational.org/co-dependency

Daxton, P. N. (2019, August 13). *How to help a narcissist heal.* Understanding Mind. https://www.understandingmind.com/how-to-help-a-narcissist-heal/

Goodman, L. (2013, June 7). *How to heal your narcissism.* The Good Men Project. https://goodmenproject.com/featured-content/how-to-heal-your-narcissism/

Henschel, C. (2014). *The effects of parenting style on the development of narcissism.* Behavioral Health. http://www.sakkyndig.com/psykologi/artvit/henschel2014.pdf

Hinders, J. (2022, March 25). *14 signs of covert abuse never to ignore.* Power of Positivity: Positive Thinking & Attitude. https://www.powerofpositivity.com/covert-abuse-signs/

How your body language influences your thinking | NeuroNation. (2015, October 29). Blog.neuronation.com. https://blog.neuronation.com/en/how-your-body-language-influences-your-thinking/

Mahadevan, N. (2021, August 9). *There are 2 types of narcissists. Here's what makes each tick.* Livescience.com. https://www.livescience.com/narcissists-what-makes-them-tick.html

Manipulation. (2019, March 26). GoodTherapy.org Therapy Blog. https://www.goodtherapy.org/blog/psychpedia/manipulation

Mayo Clinic Staff. (2017, November 18). *Narcissistic personality disorder - Symptoms and causes.* Mayo Clinic. https://www.mayoclinic.org/diseases-conditions/narcissistic-personality-disorder/symptoms-causes/syc-20366662

Miller, J. D., Campbell, W. K., & Pilkonis, P. A. (2007). *Narcissistic personality disorder: relations with distress and functional impairment.* Comprehensive Psychiatry, 48(2), 170–177. https://doi.org/10.1016/j.comppsych.2006.10.003

Nagaraj, V. (2021, February 22). *Ethical manipulation in leadership* | Psychology Today. www.psychologytoday.com. https://www.psychologytoday.com/us/blog/leading-in-the-real-world/202102/ethical-manipulation-in-leadership

Pietrangelo, A. (2020, December 11). *What therapy for narcissism involves: steps and what to expect.* Healthline. https://www.healthline.com/health/therapy-for-narcissism#types-of-therapy

Raypole, C. (2020, March 30). *Recovery from narcissistic abuse is possible — Here's how.* Healthline. https://www.healthline.com/health/mental-health/9-tips-for-narcissistic-abuse-recovery#acknowledgement

Segal, J., Smith, M., Robinson, L., & Boose, G. (2020, October). *Nonverbal communication and body language.* HelpGuide.org. https://www.helpguide.org/articles/relationships-communication/nonverbal-communication.htm

Seltzer, L. F. (2013, April 30). *A new take on manipulation* | Psychology Today. www.psychologytoday.com. https://www.psychologytoday.com/us/blog/evolution-the-self/201304/new-take-manipulation

Shahida Arabi. (2022, June 11). *20 diversion tactics highly manipulative narcissists, sociopaths and psychopaths use to silence you.* Thought Catalog; Thought Catalog. https://thoughtcatalog.com/shahida-arabi/2016/06/20-diversion-tactics-highly-manipulative-narcissists-sociopaths-and-psychopaths-use-to-silence-you/

Stines, S. (2016, October 23). *Coping with covert abuse*. Psych Central. https://psychcentral.com/pro/recovery-expert/2016/10/coping-with-covert-abuse#1

Trumpeter, N. N., Watson, P. J., O'Leary, B. J., & Weathington, B. L. (2008). *Self-Functioning and perceived parenting: Relations of parental empathy and love inconsistency with narcissism, depression, and self-esteem.* The Journal of Genetic Psychology, 169(1), 51–71. https://doi.org/10.3200/gntp.169.1.51-71

VIRZI, J. (2021, March 24). *5 kinds of childhood emotional abuse we don't talk about.* Scary Mommy. https://www.scarymommy.com/5-kinds-of-childhood-emotional-abuse

Wood MA, P. (n.d.). *Symptoms and body language of someone with narcissistic personality disorder and how their behavior may affect you* - Body Language Expert, Patti Wood, MA. www.pattiwood.net. https://www.pattiwood.net/article.asp?PageID=11796

Zajenkowski, M., & Szymaniak, K. (2019). *Narcissism between facets and domains. The relationships between two types of narcissism and aspects of the big five.* Current Psychology. https://doi.org/10.1007/s12144-019-0147-1

Made in the USA
Middletown, DE
13 June 2023

32533716R00062